JOSSEY-BASS GUIDES
TO ONLINE TEACHING AND LEARNING

Learning in Real Time

Synchronous Teaching and Learning Online

Jonathan Finkelstein

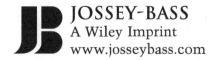

JOSSEY-BASS
A Wiley Imprint
www.josseybass.com

Published by Jossey-Bass
A Wiley Imprint
989 Market Street, San Francisco, CA 94103-1741   www.josseybass.com

Jossey-Bass books and products are available through most bookstores. To contact Jossey-Bass directly call our Customer Care Department within the U.S. at 800-956-7739, outside the U.S. at 317-572-3986, or fax 317-572-4002.

Jossey-Bass also publishes its books in a variety of electronic formats. Some content that appears in print may not be available in electronic books.

Library of Congress Cataloging-in-Publication Data

Finkelstein, Jonathan.
Learning in real time : synchronous teaching and learning online / Jonathan Finkelstein.
p. cm.
Includes bibliographical references and index.
ISBN-13: 978-0-7879-7921-8 (pbk.)
ISBN-10: 0-7879-7921-X (pbk.)
1. Computer-assisted instruction. 2. Educational technology. 3. Internet in education. 4. Distance education. 5. Education, Higher—Computer-assisted instruction. I. Title.
LB1028.5.F516 2006
371.33'4—dc22   2006010548

Printed in the United States of America
FIRST EDITION
PB Printing   10 9 8 7 6 5 4 3 2 1

Contents

For my teachers,
Mom and Dad

Preface

There is nothing new about synchronous learning. Arguably, humans have been learning in real time since they began to communicate with one another. Real-time instruction on the Internet, by comparison, is relatively new. Though many technologies are designed to remove the need for human involvement, synchronous tools turn the spotlight squarely on *people* and invite the participation of those willing, ready, and able to share, collaborate, and learn. Perhaps more than any other form of computer-mediated communication, real-time learning strips away barriers to reveal the natural give-and-take and subtleties of human dialogue that are the hallmark of in-person exchanges.

In the wake of an initial movement to seize the "anytime, anywhere" nature of the Web, bring courses online en masse, and scale enrollment, there is now a renewed focus in education on quality of instruction, student engagement, and retention. Real-time tools are playing a growing role in enhancing formal learning experiences and just-in-time interactions with instructors and peers who are increasingly connected not "*anytime,* anywhere" but "*all the time,* anywhere." Personalized and caring student support services—such as tutoring, advising, help desk, or reference support—have also been expected to meet the needs of learners who want to succeed online and are benefiting from the meaningful relationship-building and immediacy possible in synchronous settings.

The growing use of real-time technologies holds great promise to re-invent collaboration and interactivity and "warm" the way we learn online—if we choose to try new things. Regrettably, for some, their only experience in this realm has been taking part in a one-sided synchronous lecture, leaving them to question the value of real-time tools and the purpose of gathering live online. You will see few references to "slides" and "lecturing" in this book. The main thrust of the chapters that follow is to provide learning professionals with the guidance and concrete strategies needed to know *when* and *how* to facilitate synchronous interactions that leave no one wondering why everyone needed to be there at the same time.

I do not envision a world in which all learning happens in a live virtual classroom, interactive Webcast, or instant messenger. Learning happens across a continuum that includes a wide array of planned and unplanned, asynchronous and synchronous communication, and it happens in groups, one-on-one, and alone. Well-conceived, on-demand approaches that summarily exclude live interaction—whether it be formal or informal—without considering the unique possibilities it offers may be unnecessarily limiting the ultimate potential of a learning experience.

This book does envision a future in which learning that takes place in synchronous spaces resembles and builds upon the very best of offline interaction, and it serves as a needed resource to help make that so.

AUDIENCE

This book will be of great value to anyone already involved in live online teaching or facilitation, or anyone considering a foray into that realm. Each chapter considers the academic context of faculty members looking to humanize and improve learning through real-time interaction. The book will also be a valuable resource to instructional designers, tutors, advising staff, librarians, and anyone involved in faculty development, course design, or the provision of student support services. Administrators—such as those in admission, alumni, or public relations departments—may also find the book a source of inspiration for the potential of live online outreach. The instructional strategies offered here have also been successfully applied in corporate training, online marketing, and other online learning and communication arenas, and professionals in these areas will also find this book to be an important and invaluable guide.

ORGANIZATION

Intended as an accessible guidebook or desk reference, *Learning in Real Time* focuses on practical knowledge and strategies for designing and facilitating live online learning experiences. Although it draws on theoretical material, the book's emphasis is on good practice and effective use of synchronous technologies in real-world, real-time scenarios. Chapter One explores the kinds of contexts that call for live online instruction. It offers the notion of a "synchronous compact"—an implicit agreement between instructors and learners in real-time environments to focus on that which requires their concurrent presence—and asks when live interaction should be considered over asynchronous alternatives. It also highlights learner skills that can be developed and assessed uniquely in real-time settings but that are often overlooked or not taught online. Chapter Two measures the potential of synchronous learning against commonly accepted principles of good practice in education and offers first-hand evidence from practitioners in the field.

The next two chapters take a closer look at synchronous technology itself. Chapter Three examines some of the most common tools available for text, audio, and visual interaction live online and then assembles these tools into synchronous venues, such as virtual classrooms, chat rooms, instant messengers, and interactive Webcast environments, and Chapter Four explores the kinds of instructional goals best served by each.

Chapter Five turns to facilitation skills for synchronous online settings and offers seven major techniques for ensuring that learning is happening live online and that instructors are connecting effectively with students. With confidence in our ability to proficiently facilitate live activities, we proceed in Chapter Six to a set of original, instructional approaches for fostering collaboration and learning, live online. Each activity constitutes a template that can be applied to virtually any subject matter and includes several examples, variations, and suggestions for embedding the live experiences into the overall learning continuum, including asynchronous coursework.

Finally, a series of additional resources assist in scheduling synchronous events, selecting real-time tools, and justifying their use in light of common misconceptions and available alternatives. Links to Web sites that use actual, live, online tools serve as a launching pad for continued exploration and hands-on practice with the techniques presented in this book, for only real-world experience can bring about the potential of learning in real time.

ACKNOWLEDGMENTS

A very flattering invitation from Rena Palloff and Keith Pratt to write this work is what finally turned a long-standing goal into the book you are holding now. I admire Rena and Keith and thank them for their support and inspiration and for recognizing the great value offered by well-conceived, real-time online learning experiences.

I offer deep gratitude to the members of LearningTimes.org and to each and every community on the LearningTimes Network. Your selflessness, willingness to share, and warm collegiality were on my mind while composing each and every page. I thank you for the life you breathe into learning online. To the Webheads in Action, your "experiment in world friendship" through online learning is always welcome to call LearningTimes home; your energy, enthusiasm, and love for teaching and learning is anything but virtual, even if our community is.

My work on this project and on so many others benefits from closeness to creative, brilliant, and kind people such as Paul Stacey, Sivasailam "Thiagi" Thiagarajan, Lorraine Leo, Dan Balzer, Steve Gilbert, Deb Hutti, Dick Parsons, Farimah Schuerman, Amanda Majkowski, Larry Johnson, Michael Coghlan, and others. Many people call you their heroes; I am among them and am lucky to also call you my friends.

To David Brightman, my editor at Jossey-Bass, thank you and your colleagues for your confidence in me and for the opportunity to contribute to this important series of guide books.

This book would not exist were it not for my friends and colleagues at Learning-Times. In particular, I thank my friend John Walber, the consummate live producer: you are a role model, driving force, and entertaining partner in all of my work, and I cannot imagine making a living without you. And to Hope Kandel, I offer my deep respect and admiration for your talents and integrity, and your friendship. I also wish to recognize the support and guidance of Suzanne and Darrin Billig and my grandparents, all of whom I love very much.

No one bore the brunt of this project—nor deserves credit for its existence—more than Dhal Anglada. As an instructional designer and as a partner, Dhal's input into this and every undertaking is unflagging and entirely irreplaceable.

I have been fortunate to have had many great teachers in my life, and this book reflects an important contribution from each of them. But no teachers are more loved and appreciated than the two I also call Mom and Dad. Thank you, for everything.

June, 2006

Jonathan Finkelstein
New York, New York

About the Author

Jonathan Finkelstein is a pioneer in the design and use of synchronous teaching and learning tools. Few people have spent more time in real-time online learning environments facilitating and working with others to create effective learning experiences worthy of the live online medium. Jonathan created the first certification program exclusively designed for educators and trainers teaching live online. He also cofounded one of the industry's first companies creating platforms for live teaching, learning, interaction, and collaboration over the Internet. Jonathan is a frequent speaker at industry conferences and serves on several editorial and advisory boards for journals and online communities of practice that serve education professionals.

Jonathan is the founder and executive producer of LearningTimes.org and the president of the LearningTimes Network. He has been designing and producing online learning conferences, communities, events, and collaborative technologies his entire professional life. Jonathan has worked closely with a wide range of learning-focused institutions—such as the New York City Department of Education, the University of Hawaii, Ohio Learning Network, Columbia Teachers College, the Smithsonian Institution, the World Bank, Intuit, MetLife, and the American Library Association—

to grow and maintain online learning communities and foster human interaction live online. Many of his online programs and applications have been recognized with industry awards.

As the executive producer of LearningTimes.org, a free, worldwide community for education and training, Jonathan helps craft a variety of online forums, both live and asynchronous, in which education professionals collaborate and learn from peers and industry leaders. Jonathan has also led the formation and growth of the LearningTimes Network, a rapidly growing series of interconnected online learning communities, all of which feature opportunities for formal and impromptu live online interaction and collaboration. The LearningTimes Network connects education-minded organizations of all kinds, fostering partnerships among educational institutions, associations, corporate entities, museums, and other groups whose missions include reaching a global audience of learners.

The son of two New York City public school teachers, Jonathan is a Certified Synchronous Training Professional (CSTP) and received his A.B. degree cum laude from Harvard University.

Learning in Real Time

Learning, Live Online

With mounting experience in the online environment, an increasing number of learning professionals are now ready to find ways to add life, and the magic of real-time interaction, back into the learning process. In the vast movement to transition campus-based experiences to the online realm, the immediacy and value of live interaction have often been sacrificed to a perception that the Web is no place for anything that is not "anytime, anywhere." Though "anytime" or asynchronous modes of communication have been an empowering factor in allowing learners to transcend traditional limits of place and time, not every learning objective or need can be met in the absence of real-time human interaction.

Situations that call for proximity to others, even figuratively, are found all across the learning continuum from collaboration to skills development to community-building or just-in-time support. Learning environments that have shied away from any form of real-time interaction may be unnecessarily limiting the overall potential of what each student can learn, and what the institution can offer.

Rapid improvements in technology and Internet connectivity, coupled with increasing comfort levels and support in using basic online communication and learning tools, have impelled educators to tap back into the fostering of relationships with students in real time that have been the hallmark of their on-campus teaching experience. Most important, a renewed focus on the quality of instruction and student engagement that has followed the first wave of online learning (Palloff and Pratt, 2005) inevitably means a greater consideration of tools that humanize the learning experience, efficiently teach and gauge performance-based skills, and cultivate natural means for collaborating and learning in real time.

SYNCHRONOUS INTERACTION ACROSS THE LEARNING CONTINUUM

Perceived by many as merely a means to deliver formal instruction or lectures online, real-time or *synchronous* venues actually play a much broader role across the entire learning continuum. In physical settings, live conversations and real-time human interaction are the lifeblood of academic life and adult learning. Remove from the equation things such as

- Unplanned chats among peers over lunch
- Lively in-class discussions or debates
- Student-led presentations or performances
- Study group, team, or committee gatherings
- Hallway conversations with classmates or colleagues
- Impromptu exchanges between a student and instructor after class or during office hours
- Timely and personalized guidance from a reference librarian, advisor, or coach
- Serendipitous meetings on campus

and what remains are course materials, reading assignments, and isolated, independent study—none of which provide the kind of supportive, dynamic, and human environment that helps learners be engaged, motivated, or successful. If the first wave of moving courses online has taught us anything, it is that opportunities for interaction and collaboration are crucial elements of successful learning environments. Not considering opportunities to add human interaction—in any form—to online programs or courses summarily dismisses a vital form of communication for learning, skill development, support, and community-building.

NEEDS SERVED BY SYNCHRONOUS INTERACTION

Although consideration of synchronous interaction might first turn to instructor-led activities or lessons, real-time interaction and learning can take as many forms and happen in about as many different kinds of contexts *online* as it does in our physical learning settings. At least five major functions are served by real-time, online interaction within a learning environment:

- Instruction
- Collaboration
- Support
- Socialization and informal exchange
- Extended outreach

Instruction encompasses any of the kinds of learning that happen when faculty members, knowledge experts, or facilitators meet with learners, usually in a planned manner in a specific online venue, to guide them through the achievement of learning objectives. This is a very broad category, and there are at least as many methods and pedagogical approaches to engage in live online instruction as there are in any other setting, online or off. Nonetheless, this book places a greater emphasis on an active or constructivist (Piaget, 1969) approach to instruction within synchronous settings. People need not be present concurrently with an instructor to simply have information passed on to them, yet the active construction of knowledge by learners through a process of real-time give-and-take is well-served in a live online setting.

Collaboration is a key element to the success of an online learning environment (Conrad and Donaldson, 2004). It is also, as I discuss later, a skill that has become part of a global working environment. Although the presence of a facilitator can guide collaborative activities, these interactions tend to be more egalitarian in nature and can happen at any time, in both structured and informal settings, with two or more people present. Live online settings offer an immediacy that not only allows collaboration to begin instantaneously but also contracts the actual time spent on task.

Support is a crucial element for retaining and motivating learners, whether it is provided by just-in-time assistance from a peer, instructor, tutor, advisor, or librarian. No other form of online communication can give personalized human support faster or at the moment it is most needed than a live exchange with the right person.

Socialization and informal exchanges are activities whose contributions to the learning process are most difficult to quantify. Interactions in this realm often dispense with formality and can even be short of substance, yet without them a crucial foundation on which to build instructional activities is lacking. The proliferation of instant messengers, online chat rooms, and mobile messaging in social contexts (Shiu and Lenhart, 2004) alone affirms that live online venues are an increasingly common and comfortable form of live interaction. In learning environments, they help build community and create a friendly and safe environment in which people can feel like people.

Extended outreach is an important aspect of any institution's connection to the world beyond its gates. Admission information sessions, alumni relations, online conferences, multicampus professional development, and lifelong education programs are among the many reasons for the use of synchronous online communication outside of the formal instructional arena.

Various Purposes, Various Venues

There are almost as many online tools and venues for synchronous interaction as there are activities that call for their use. With instant messengers, chat rooms, online reference desks, interactive Webcasting platforms, and virtual classrooms, offices, and meeting rooms there is no shortage of available options to meet and interact live online. The ultimate question is what we do in these spaces that helps us achieve communication and learning objectives not realized as ideally in any other manner.

Why Live?

When it comes to instruction, course content and communication can be channeled through many forums and formats. The online environment offers a vast array of permutations for interacting and sharing knowledge with students. E-mail, discussion threads, Web resources, blogs, online reading materials, and recorded audio or video are just a few of the more common means to reach learners online. With so many tools and media formats available, the choice to "go live" online should be a deliberate one based on what can uniquely be accomplished when people congregate in real time. A successful real-time, online learning experience begins with a clear and confident answer to the question: *Why live?*

A prerequisite to the effective use of synchronous tools is that the decision to use these tools was made to support a cause worthy of the live medium. If the purpose can better be achieved through the dissemination of a document, via a link to a recorded lecture, or by a simple e-mail to students, it should. Synchronous learning should be deployed when synchronous learning is uniquely suited. Not adhering to this basic principle can damage learners' trust in an instructor's instructional prerogatives and dampen learner motivation.

THE SYNCHRONOUS COMPACT

Live online experiences must start with an implicit or even explicit compact or agreement between an instructor or facilitator and participating learners. In this "synchronous compact," learners agree to minimize the distractions they have around them and to make every effort to contribute meaningfully to the experience. The instructor's half of this bargain is to remember at every moment of every live session that there is a group of people assembled in real time who have set aside the same precious hour out of their day and to make every effort to use the time together in a manner that takes advantage of the fact that all are present in real time.

Meeting the Threshold to Go Live

In deciding whether or not to call for a live online session, it is extremely instructional to ask one's self: "Why am I asking my group to all login at, say, 3:00 P.M. on a Wednesday? Why is it important that they all stop what they are doing to take the same exact hour to be online together with me or with each other? In light of all my available options, why is this the right way to go?" The lack of an answer that is compelling to you or that would be to your learners should be an immediate indicator to reconsider the alternatives. The full potential of any learning experience cannot be achieved when learners are led to ponder, *Tell me again, why am I here?*

New Opportunities

In addressing these questions and moving instructional experiences online, exciting new opportunities exist to rethink and improve upon old paradigms. One such tradition, for example, is the live lecture, which has been "baked" into the academic structure of most institutions for centuries. Taking a course—or aspects of a course—online need not be seen as requiring a direct translation of the thrice-weekly lecture to the online realm. The evolution of instructional design to include the use of synchronous online tools offers a great impetus to reinvent how instructors spend time with learners.

Using a real-time environment to lecture learners can be an expedient use of a virtual classroom environment, but it neglects some of the most creative possibilities of a tool that essentially "wires" all learners to the instructor and to each other. Such "connected" learning—the combined use of real-time polling, drawing, annotation, text chat, Web exploration, rich media, and visual, voice, and video tools with two or more people online—can open the door to new and unique ways to achieve learning objectives.

The synchronous realm of learning offers a variety of unique attributes, such as

- Immediate and just-in-time access to peers, instructors, and knowledge experts
- The ability for multiple people to interact and share ideas with one another concurrently
- Hands-on tools through which learners can react to presented concepts or apply knowledge in real time
- Direct connections to real-world situations and primary resources
- The means to demonstrate and assess real-time skills and analytical thinking
- The ability to include a more diverse learner population in real-time discussions
- The capacity to bridge guest expertise into the learning environment

The unique potential of synchronous instruction and real-time communication online must be recognized if the tools are going to be used effectively and truly make a difference in learner outcomes. Despite the growing use of synchronous tools in instruction, many years of experience suggest that the tools are still seen primarily as a means to replicate traditional, campus-based instructional activities—for good or bad—rather than to explore new avenues of improving student learning. An uninspired slide lecture delivered on campus will be at least as unappealing in the online environment, where the learner's opportunities for distraction are greater.

Real-time, online instructional tools hold great promise. At their core is the potential to expose online learners, even at great distances, to the impassioned understanding and the contagious appreciation that instructors, and often peers, bring to the subject at hand.

The presence of a live instructor, combined with the use of the human voice and a rich set of facilitation and collaboration possibilities, opens up a new world for those who love to teach and who know that fostering moments of epiphany often requires the presence and real-time give-and-take of a guide present at one's side. The use of synchronous tools among peers for both informal and formal instructional activities personalizes learning and provides a needed support framework. It is also closer in many ways to the mode of interaction through which many learners will need to apply their education in their professional lives, where demonstrating knowledge will often happen on the fly and via effective communication that will not always be asynchronous. I will discuss the role played by real-time environments in developing these kinds of learner skills in the next chapter.

INDICATORS FOR REAL-TIME ONLINE LEARNING

What are some of the indicators that a live online interaction may be the preferred means for communicating with learners online?

• *Lessons are best learned from group discussion or collaboration.* For an instructor, few things are as rewarding as watching the exploration of a topic take flight as learners discuss, collaborate, construct knowledge, and work together to solve problems. Many live online environments are well suited for this kind of learning experience and often offer greater efficiency than asynchronous alternatives. There are times when a real-time dialogue that unfolds over a five-minute period might take five days in an asynchronous format. Shades of meaning that are misinterpreted in asynchronous interactions and send groups on unnecessary tangents are resolved quickly in real time, and more relevant ground is covered.

• *Sparking deeper appreciation for and understanding of the subject matter is desired.* A good instructor not only teaches but also inspires. In offline settings, that inspiration is often conveyed through the conviction of the human voice, spirited explanations, and impassioned gestures. Spontaneity, humor, and direct invitations to engage learners in the here and now of discussion are all ingredients for the kind of contagious enthusiasm that arouses a learner's deeper understanding and appreciation for the subject matter at hand. Real-time learning tools help expedite the generation of these sparks.

• *A safe environment for exploration and sharing and a sense of community are vital to achieving learning objectives.* The proper exploration of some topics relies on candid dialogue and sharing among learners. Ethics, counseling, politics, and nursing are but a few disciplines in which learners are often asked to share their personal opinions, biases, and feelings. A sense of community—where members of a group trust each other and their facilitator and feel willing and comfortable enough to contribute—can help expedite sharing activities. Live online settings can be safe places to quickly and efficiently build that sense of community and cooperation.

• *Learning involves the rehearsal, demonstration, and assessment of particular skills.* Whether it be oral communication, analytical thinking, real-time problem solving, software proficiency, information literacy, or any number of performance-based skills, real-time venues afford opportunities to provide instruction and assess learner aptitudes in ways that are highly impractical, if not impossible, in an asynchronous manner.

• *Information is complex and guidance is necessary.* A knowledgeable instructor can walk learners through material that is difficult to absorb independently and teach them methods for deciphering complex information they may encounter later on their own.

• *There is a need to adjust the level or complexity of material on-the-fly based on learner feedback.* Learners can come to the table with an uneven understanding of the material before them. Even when official course prerequisites have been satisfied, good instructors often gauge the comfort level of their learners with the level of the material being taught and then adjust their lesson and approaches accordingly. The efficiency with which this kind of adaptation can happen in a real-time environment often exceeds what can be done in any other online format.

• *Comprehension must be ensured before learning proceeds.* Real-time interaction with learners can often yield a better assessment of learner comprehension than a formal evaluative instrument, such as a quiz, survey, or homework assignment. Observing in real time things such as the amount of time it takes a learner to respond to a question, the degree of self-confidence in a spontaneously crafted response, the reliance of the learner on third-party supports in explaining a concept, or the accuracy of the underlying thought process revealed by watching or listening as a problem is solved are all subtle yet powerful instructional techniques much more readily put to use in synchronous online situations than asynchronous ones. Merely getting an answer correct—as one might do by luck on an exam—does not mean that the learner grasps the concept. Real-time online interaction with students can draw out the true level of comprehension and shore up cracks in the foundation on which future lessons will depend.

• *Questions and trouble spots cannot necessarily be predicted.* No amount of advance preparation can allow one to predict all questions that learners will have when they review course material. A live online session takes the guesswork out of knowing learner trouble spots and allows for an efficient real-time response to keep learners on track. The presence of an instructor in real time to aid learners at exactly the point they might otherwise get frustrated and quit can lead to improved learner retention and outcomes.

• *Information is fast-changing.* Many disciplines see innovation and change overnight. To keep these courses relevant and compelling to learners—even within the context of a semester-long course—an instructor often wants to bring current events, news, or information into his or her online courses. The agenda for technology, economics, or political science courses grounded in current events or practices, for example, can morph in an instant. Preparing asynchronous materials to describe new concepts in such short time frames can be overwhelming or unwieldy. Real-time tools can provide a suitable alternative, allowing the instructor to orchestrate discussions of late-breaking information with learners in a less formal context than prepared, standalone materials or asynchronous exchanges might require.

• *Ensuring participation and improving learner retention is paramount.* There is nothing like knowing that a real person is waiting at a specific time to conduct a class—and is expecting your attendance and participation—to motivate online learners and get them to show up and participate. As a retention and motivation tool, live online sessions can "anchor" an overall learning program and provide achievable milestone moments that keep a learner engaged and progressing through a course or workshop. How many of us have shown up for a class because we did not want to let down an instructor? Interactive, live sessions can also help those learners who are disinclined to self-paced exploration or who do best when led by the hand through new material. The increased comfort level that comes from working together with an instructor or in a group can be the difference between sinking out at sea alone or swimming to the safety of understanding and course completion.

• *A guest expert is available to interact with learners for a limited time.* Instructors who enhance their courses by securing participation from a guest expert may find that their subject matter specialist can only commit to a brief "appearance." Rather than ask the expert for the kind of ongoing or open-ended commitment that might characterize participation in a discussion board, an instructor might use a real-time interactive forum and consolidate the guest's interaction with students to a set hour on a specific day.

• *Dialogue or debate among learners is required.* Observing and participating in debate or dialogue with instructors or peers who have different perspectives or opinions can be a meaningful aspect of a learning experience. Few course communication options can convey or allow the immediacy and spontaneity of debate that synchronous tools offer.

• *Distance-based learners and campus-based learners need access to the same experts.* Hybrid courses that simultaneously serve on-campus and distance-based students can make good use of real-time communication tools to bridge classroom-based experiences to remote learners. If the right tools are selected and deployed wisely, distance-based students can enjoy just as much interaction with instructors, peers, and guest experts as their on-campus counterparts.

• *The situation calls for personal, real-time attention.* Some learning situations simply call for interaction that is as human as humanly possible. Reacting to a learner's present state and concerns and providing encouragement, support, and reinforcement appropriate for the moment of need are skills more aptly dispensed by a person in real time than in a time-shifted manner or by a computer program. Certainly, the expression of humanity within a course is not purely the domain of synchronous environments. But when it comes to allowing instructors to behave naturally, convey their sense of humor, tell stories, express themselves vocally, lend a listening ear, or use other subtleties of human communication to connect with learners, real-time online environments most closely resemble the physical spaces traditionally home to such personal forms of expression.

LEARNER SKILLS DEVELOPED AND ASSESSED LIVE ONLINE

Much attention is given to the kinds of *content* that are suitable for learning in synchronous environments, but real-time venues are also uniquely suited places for the learning, practicing, and assessing of certain performance-based *skills*. Sometimes these skills are the primary purpose of a synchronous interaction; other times they are beneficial byproducts or outgrowths of exploration of a topic at hand. Many of these learner aptitudes are difficult to teach or measure without the concurrent presence of both learner and instructor, and often peers as well, especially when collaborative techniques are being gauged.

Assessing Skills and Abilities

The most common methods of assessment in higher education today are traditional approaches such as problem-based examinations or essays (Juwah, 2003), which do not "adequately test for imponderables like independent critical thinking, creativity" (Elton and Johnston, 2002, p. 7), confidence, performance, or oral mastery. In the online realm, this has not changed significantly, although one trend toward electronic portfolios or e-portfolios—the collecting and assessing of a body of student work rather than one particular exam or assignment—is showing promise in some institutions. E-portfolios can provide a more holistic and richer view of student achievement and development, which aids in learner evaluation (Chen and Mazow, 2002). Although some e-portfolios do incorporate rich media such as audio and video projects created by students, the approach is still asynchronous in nature and therefore excludes the portrayal of those student accomplishments and skills that are performed in real time or that require the presence of others to adequately demonstrate.

An assessment of abilities needed by learners to succeed in today's world offered by the Partnership for 21st Century Skills suggests that real-time collaboration, learning, and interaction can help advance the cause of skill development across a range of categories, such as "global awareness," "interpersonal learning," and "information and communication technology (ICT)." This is not to say that the use of synchronous tools is the only method to prepare our learners with skills essential for success in today's workplaces and communities, but they are undeniably well-suited and should be seriously considered as we craft learning experiences that prepare students for today's real-world challenges. This book's companion Web site (www.learninginrealtime.com) includes an excerpt from the twenty-first century skills report of some of the specific performance-based abilities that are well-served by real-time online activities.

Skills Assessed Uniquely Live Online

In very concrete terms, there are some aptitudes or skill areas for which training or assessment by any other means would be artificial, inefficient, or simply impossible. Here are some skills and situations for which many synchronous environments seem tailor-made:

- Public speaking or presentation skills
- Real-time problem solving and analytical thinking
- Listening and reading comprehension in native and second languages
- Composure in reflecting and responding under pressure
- Well-reasoned conversations on discipline-specific topics; offering cogent responses in a timely manner
- Persuasive, well-articulated, and well-spoken oral arguments; practicing the art of oral rhetoric
- Storytelling skills
- Debate
- Proficiency in software skills or other real-time applications or processes
- Demonstration of how certain results are achieved in math or accounting or other fields where it is essential to be able to "show your work" and consciously replicate results
- Appropriate speech with clients, colleagues, or patients exhibiting proper etiquette or bedside manner
- Effective use of one's voice to convey shades of meaning or to perform, such as with music, in drama, or poetry
- Fluency in a second language, including proper pronunciation
- Immediate application of material learned to real-world problems or contexts
- Role-play in simulated situations in preparation for real-world scenarios

- Comfort and competence in ICT skills for collaboration and communication
- Ability to work well and collaborate with others in team activities
- Demonstrated leadership skills in developing, fluid situations

Although they are appearing increasingly and with great success, the teaching and gauging of performance-based skills like these are still relatively rare among the body of courses currently online. Courses or entire programs may not even be considered for online delivery when learning objectives include the need for the development, demonstration, or mastery of such skills. Sometimes this is because instructors still lack access to real-time online tools that would support performance-based instruction and assessment, or they may be unaware of the potential of synchronous venues. Although understandably we may be wary of visiting a surgeon whose entire repertoire was learned online, mounting experience in real-time online venues suggests that as instructors we should be open to the great capacity that these tools offer for teaching collaborative, communication, problem-solving, and other vital twenty-first century skills online.

Real-Time Learning as Good Practice

Responding to a series of reports released in the early 1980s calling for reforms in U.S. higher education, Arthur Chickering and Zelda Gamson composed "Seven Principles for Good Practice in Undergraduate Education" (1987). The principles quickly became a fixture in faculty and administrative offices across North America and beyond, thanks in part to their "jargon-free" (Chickering and Ehrmann, 2003) approach to simplifying years of academic research and faculty experience into a few memorable core tenets of good instruction.

Although the drafting of these guiding principles predates the Internet's revolutionary impact on education, it is a testament to their aphoristic nature and timeless relevance that they are still cited widely today in the context of crafting quality online learning experiences. Trends in online learning toward more interactive, facilitator-led coursework, versus the off-the-shelf, self-paced modules that epitomized the earliest forms of computer-based education, suggest that the truths suggested by Chickering and Gamson may be increasingly self-evident to instructors and learners alike—and not just in undergraduate education but anywhere formal learning opportunities are being offered. According to Chickering and Gamson (1987), good practice

1. Encourages contact between students and faculty
2. Develops reciprocity and cooperation among students
3. Encourages active learning
4. Gives prompt feedback
5. Emphasizes time on task
6. Communicates high expectations
7. Respects diverse talents and ways of learning

Evaluating an online course or program by how well it adheres to these principles of good practice can be a productive exercise and produce useful insights into how to improve instruction (Graham and others, 2001). Although live online learning activities rarely live in isolation of a broader context—namely, at least some forms of asynchronous communication or on-demand resources—it is still instructive to examine how the realm of real-time online interaction and collaboration can advance what are now generally accepted standards of good practice in education.

We will now look at each principle—together with some specific faculty examples of good practice—to glean what synchronous communication offers in the way of advancing the cause of a quality educational experience.

CONTACT BETWEEN STUDENTS AND FACULTY

Good practice encourages student-faculty contact.

—A. Chickering and Z. Gamson (1987)

In the online environment, there is no more direct or immediate means to connect students and their instructors than through synchronous interaction. In a summary of studies conducted in this arena, Shauna Schullo of the University of South Florida points out that "research in distance learning continues to emphasize the importance of interaction for effective teaching" (2003). During well-facilitated, real-time online class sessions, instructors are able to actively encourage involvement and motivate learners. An instructor well attuned to the students assembled will be able to spot the struggling learners and help them get back up on their feet before the world passes them by.

Formal or planned synchronous class activities are but one approach to fostering contact between teacher and learner. With the proliferation of real-time presence software such as free text– and audio-based instant messengers, student-faculty contact can happen at any time from virtually anywhere. No longer must the power of real-time interaction be confined to scheduled class lessons taking place as a full group at a specific time in a chat room or virtual classroom. Instructor accessibility—whether or not learners avail themselves of it—conveys a sense of caring for students' well-being that is assuring and motivating for many learners. Michael Coghlan, an educator and e-learning coordinator from Adelaide, South Australia, describes the nature and outcome of remote real-time exchanges with one of his students in Taiwan:

> Ying Lan and I used to meet regularly via instant messenger for voice chats. Ying was a student of mine in one of the free English for the Internet (EFI) courses. It was around 1998—a time when there were few courses of instruction about how to teach on the Web—and we were all carving out our own methodologies.
>
> Ying Lan worked in a bank in Taiwan, and her work occasionally required her to work with English speaking foreigners. Apart from this she had no contact with native English speakers, and so she turned to EFI for help with speaking and listening in English. Using the voice capability of the instant messenger, together Ying and I worked on her speaking and listening skills. She would bring words and phrases to practice at the meeting and she would listen to my pronunciation and repeat the words and phrases as often as was necessary to get the pronunciation right. I noticed a marked improvement in her pronunciation within weeks.
>
> A neat coda to this story is that Ying's dedication to learning English on the Internet eventually won her a position with her bank where she was stationed in the U.S. for a year. (Coghlan, personal communication, June 14, 2005)

The ability to deliver on this good practice in the age of near-ubiquitous, just-in-time communication tools is not in doubt. If anything, instructors (or their students) may need to set reasonable expectations regarding when they will or will not engage in dialogue "outside of class"—a notion whose lines are difficult to define in a world where the "classroom" lights are always on. Nonetheless, since our main objective as educators is helping our students learn, succeed, and tap into their own motivation, too much interaction is arguably a better problem to have than not enough or none at all. It is often easier to set limits and pare down communication with engaged and energized learners if necessary than to expend the energy needed to rescue learners who fall off the radar or drop out entirely.

COOPERATION AMONG STUDENTS

Good practice encourages cooperation among students.

—A. Chickering and Z. Gamson (1987)

The Internet is designed for communication and collaboration, and the advent of the World Wide Web and its rapid adoption into the world of education has opened up many possibilities for enabling cooperation among students. The use of synchronous tools is an efficient means to build a sense of community and foster a sharing spirit among students, who may interact with each other in the context of a formal live class activity or in one-on-one or smaller group gatherings. A quality online course encourages students to learn together in community, and as Rena Palloff and Keith Pratt remind us, "the likelihood of successful achievement of learning objectives and achieving course competencies increases through collaborative engagement"(2005, p. 8).

Peer Collaboration Models Skills Needed in the Real World

Cooperative learning among peers in real time—regardless of the discipline under discussion—also provides opportunities to learn and practice important skills needed for success in today's workplace. In completely distance-based programs, learners may rely heavily on their educational institutions to furnish opportunities to hone skills—not just content knowledge—that they will be expected to possess in order to advance in their professional lives. A British government report offering an assessment of skills needed in the modern workplace cites a growing tendency toward team-working and reduced supervision at work, and the concomitant need for workers to communicate and listen well to colleagues and customers in order to succeed (Pumphrey and Slater, 2002). If this kind of real-world business communication only happened asynchronously, it might be appropriate to teach it solely in an asynchronous manner. But despite or perhaps because of the proliferation in computer-mediated communication throughout the workplace, competence in real-time protocols, analytical thinking, and collaboration are must-have skills, and academic programs must consider their responsibility to produce learners who possess them.

Informal Learning Opportunities

The unplanned or unstructured interactions that take place when peers decide to meet live online constitute a form of incidental and informal learning, which may be the most pervasive kind of adult learning (Marsick and Watkins, 2001). Anyone who works in an academic environment or has studied in one knows that more of our learning happens over lunch in the cafeteria, in conversations with our colleagues, or in one-on-one dialogues with coaches, librarians, or mentors than in scheduled classes or activities. One great challenge for those planning online learning—especially in completely distance-based environments—is to create and foster opportunities for learners to effortlessly fall into settings and situations where they can interact informally with one another.

To that end, most online course venues support the creation of designated group areas to facilitate real-time and asynchronous teamwork, and these virtual spaces increasingly include access to more advanced text- and audio-based meeting rooms. The availability of a real-time group space gives students the option to plan to meet at mutually convenient times to collaborate on team projects. Furthermore, teammates can decide in an ad hoc manner to move into a live meeting room for unscheduled interaction. It is not uncommon for students posting messages to asynchronous discussion boards to realize that many of their peers are logged in and posting at the same time, often sharing thoughts that are redundant or at odds because they are crossing each other in cyberspace. Students will spontaneously decide to congregate in a real-time room or via instant messenger to discuss their project without the often inefficient, overlapping back-and-forth that can characterize their threaded forum conversations.

Instructors Are Also Served When Students Cooperate with One Another

While the learner's education is well-served through peer cooperation, the instructor also benefits from community-based instruction. With students far outnumbering course facilitators, it can become an unintended burden for an instructor to respond, in real time or otherwise, to each and every question that is posed by learners. If students are invited or asked to turn to each other for guidance, interaction proceeds without one person being the limiting factor, learners feel less isolated, and instructors can focus on the quality of interaction rather than being encumbered by the quantity of it.

Assessing Group Work Conducted Live Online

Instructors who usually monitor discussion boards to gauge contributions during group projects may be concerned that the use of synchronous tools by students eliminates the "tracks" they would normally leave behind in an asynchronous forum. One approach that does not discourage students from self-organizing in synchronous gatherings, yet still provides a measurable record of their process, is asking that a representative from any team that chooses to meet live online post a brief text summary in the team's asynchronous discussion area. This, as can be explained to them, not only helps ensure that they get proper credit for their "outside" work but also affords experience in good practice in the workplace. Meeting minutes serve as a useful historical record and help those who could not participate stay up to date. An instructor could also maintain or ask students to save a transcript or recording of all text or audio-based meetings, but in some cases this may discourage a candid, productive dialogue among students.

Facilitating Environments for Sharing and Cooperation

In Chapter Six you will find several detailed examples of synchronous practices that encourage learners to work in groups to achieve learning objectives. Some synchronous activities are completely left to students to organize; others make use of a real-time facilitator to foster an atmosphere of community, sharing, and learning. Here is an anecdote from an educator in Australia that exemplifies the latter scenario, and it involves students doing postgraduate studies in professional management:

> The Australian Institute of Management (AIM) offers a Graduate Certificate in Professional Management which is part of an overall MBA.

This program has traditionally been delivered in face-to-face and distant education modes, but earlier this year went live with an online mode as well. Seven students around Queensland made up the initial cohort, with the facilitator based in Brisbane. The course used "traditional" online asynchronous tools to support the students, but twice a week, the facilitator employed an audio-based virtual meeting room product to offer live online sessions meant to allow the students to reflect on the course with one another.

The feedback from the cohort was extremely positive. Due to the nature of this program, the students were all senior managers running small business, government organisations, or regional departments of larger corporate organisations. All of them were time poor, yet extremely self-motivated individuals, who, due to their disparate locations, cherished the opportunity to share in real-time their experiences as managers for their respective organisations. We discovered that the reflection which occurred during the sessions was beyond the expectations of many of the participants who were using this technology for the first time. (G. Beevers, personal communication, June 12, 2005)

Real-time discussion—with its immediacy and ability to offer shades of meaning through the subtlety and range of the human voice—can be a warm, safe, and supportive environment for deepening learners' understanding of a common subject and the unique perspectives of those who study it with them.

ACTIVE LEARNING

> *Good practice encourages active learning.*
>
> —A. Chickering and Z. Gamson (1987)

This principle is a proxy for a large body of work that convincingly makes the case for learner-centered approaches in which students are actively engaged in the process of constructing their own knowledge, rather than having it transferred to them through rote memorization or a virtual intravenous tube. Rita-Marie Conrad and J. Ana Donaldson, in building on the foundational learner-centered and constructivist conclusions of the likes of Dewey, Piaget, Bruner, Vygostky, and Knowles, among numerous others, exhort us to remember that in *online* courses, learners must be "active knowledge-generators" and must "assume responsibility for constructing and managing their own learning experience" (2004, p. 7).

Real-time learning environments invite active learning. It is their *raison d'être.* As Coghlan reports, they are "designed for dialogue" and "participants in synchronous events typically want to do more than serve as a passive audience" (2004a). Without the engaged and active involvement of learners, synchronous venues are empty vessels, echo chambers, or lecterns. Yet active learning does not just happen. An environment where it is encouraged needs to be supported and the process needs to be modeled by instructors who see a live online venue more as a learning laboratory than as a lecture hall.

Chapter Six offers specific activities for real-time use and explores many active learning approaches, such as live cracker barrels, student-led lessons, and brainstorming activities. But let us take a look at one real-world, real-time example that leverages both the learners' active involvement and the presence of a facilitator to construct an experience that the learners clearly own. The live session was aimed at helping learners become power searchers of digital resources, and it was led by Dan Balzer in an audio-based virtual classroom with about twenty-five participants. Balzer elaborates:

> My intended outcomes for the session were twofold: provide a comfortable space to test the participants' search skills and give performance-oriented feedback based on our research that would make them more effective searchers of the Internet and other online databases. So, we built the session around an "Internet Search Challenge." Everyone was given ten minutes during the session to use Google to find a specific website that answered the question: "What was the temperature in New York City on February 20, 1999?" After the Search Challenge, participants shared their search strategies. Some participants had found the URL quickly, while others had become frustrated as they discovered the limits of their search skills. Then, using the desktop sharing tool, we showed them how an expert would conduct that search. We followed this feedback with another Search Challenge so they could apply the tips and refine their skills. Unlike an asynchronous experience, the

synchronous classroom allowed us to engage the learners at their own desktops to provide real-time, guided practice for a common everyday task. In one hour we were able to move the participants through a powerful learning cycle: Search Challenge, Feedback, Search Challenge. (Balzer, 2005)

This example shows how a live environment can stimulate active learning, in turn helping learners develop better problem-solving skills, and equipping them with knowledge they can put to use immediately outside the live class context.

PROMPT FEEDBACK

Good practice gives prompt feedback.

—A. Chickering and Z. Gamson (1987)

Instantaneous is probably the fastest form of *prompt,* and synchronous communication is nothing if not instantaneous. There's no time for pacing across the room, no hourly refreshing of a discussion board, and no nervous week-long stretches while you cross your fingers and wonder how your contributions will be received. In real-time learning environments, learners know *now.* And when they get instructor feedback *now,* they can immediately absorb it into their understanding and begin to build upon it, or they can take issue with it and instantly seek and receive more feedback, thus creating an experience that constantly builds upon itself.

Good synchronous experiences do just that: they build. Of course learning that is not live can also grow and evolve to new levels; it just takes longer. Synchronous interaction, especially that which is well facilitated, offers an opportunity to respond in subtle ways, offering prompt feedback that steers a learning experience in just the desired direction.

Prompt Feedback Maintains Interest and Keeps Learners Engaged

Research and experience tell us that prompt feedback is important in online learning settings, where students lack many of the traditional nonverbal cues to which they are accustomed in face-to-face venues. Without immediate feedback, students report feeling isolated and unsatisfied (McIsaac, Blocher, Mahes, and Vrasidas, 1999). Joel Haefner, in suggesting that asynchronous communication alone cannot offer the kind of immediacy that is sometimes required for successful learning experiences to unfold, says: "If it takes days, or even hours, for students to get a response to a question, many students will lose the intellectual thread—and the urge to follow it" (2000).

Synchronous tools offer a wide range of opportunities for students to receive instantaneous feedback, both in scheduled events and in just-in-time interactions with their instructors. For example:

- An instructor visually and orally "walks through" the editing of a paper in real time, providing a window into the thought process by which student work is assessed and offering learners the immediate opportunity to elaborate on their own thinking and to ask follow-up questions to the critiques in order to improve their work.

- A student working on a research paper sees that her instructor is connected on instant messenger and asks a quick question to confirm whether she is on the right path. The instructor affirms her direction or steers her accordingly, and the student returns to her project.

- While using a virtual whiteboard to solve a math problem, a student is interrupted by a live online instructor who suggests stepping back for a moment to see whether something does not look right. The student pauses and realizes he made an erroneous assumption, corrects it, and is back on track.

Prompt Feedback Builds Momentum

Feedback is not always about merely getting an answer to one question or finding out how you did on a paper or exam. Immediacy is bi-directional. When a student gets a reaction from an instructor or peers in real time, she has the opportunity to take things a step further, question, prod, or reflect and advance the dialogue. In quality synchronous sessions, this kind of feedback is happening continuously and affords an instructor the opening to let things unfold in unscripted, yet quite meaningful ways. This kind of spontaneity and rich feedback cycle is well illustrated by an anecdote from Michael Hosking, who uses synchronous tools to tutor math and science students online.

As a supplement to archived instruction, we hold two live "office hours" per week using a Web conferencing tool. In a recent biology office hours session, we began discussing the immune system. I asked the students about the major differences between bacteria and viruses. The session quickly took us through a series of interconnected topics, following this totally unscripted path:

- Discussed the notion of life versus non-life; viruses are not technically alive. (We drew on the virtual dry erase board the structure of viruses and bacteria.)
- Talked about the ubiquity of microorganisms.
- Imagined living as humans before we knew that microorganisms existed and were related to disease.
- Touched on the invention of the microscope, with a discussion of Leeuwenhoek.
- Did a quick Web search for sites on Leeuwenhoek, with all of us sharing and reading interesting "finds" together using the application sharing tool.
- Moved on to an in-depth discussion of the Black Plague in Europe (1348) followed by another Web Quest for Black Plague sites and shared viewing.
- Returned to the virtual dry erase board so I could draw a graph of human population before and after the Plague, graphically representing how fully one-third of the human population died. A discussion of the exponential growth curve ensued, which we had covered in prior sessions.
- A posting of a link to a Black Plague site in the discussion forum after the office hour ended so that students who did not attend live could see what we discussed.

All of these individual connections followed naturally and spontaneously from the overall topic and can be viewed as a pathway through a three-dimensional space of related concepts. We use the Web as a communication tool for learning, one that allows the sort of real-time adaptive assessment of a student's understanding, with immediate and context-dependent feedback, that no software program or text content can provide. (Hosking, personal commuication, June 8, 2005)

TIME ON TASK

Good practice emphasizes time on task.

—A. Chickering and Z. Gamson (1987)

There is perhaps no better way to emphasize time on task than by modeling it for students, and facilitating a live online session in a manner that is worthy of everyone's concurrent presence and that values each participant's time does just that. Starting a planned live session on schedule, using the limited time together efficiently and productively, and keeping everyone's focus on achieving stated objectives demonstrates an approach that not only serves students well within a live event but can also be employed when they tackle their individual work.

A decision to ask learners to gather in real time online should involve consideration as to what will be accomplished while live online that could not be accomplished as or more efficiently by an asynchronous means. We do not emphasize time on task by making our learners listen to us read lecture notes live online, but we do risk losing their respect by not respecting their time. Similarly, allowing students who did not test their computers in advance of a synchronous session to disrupt the first twenty minutes of a live lesson or conducting a lengthy ice breaker exercise when there is no ice to be broken are not good ways to model time on task. When we lead synchronous activities, we can demonstrate and set the tone for a good work ethic within the learning environment.

Anchor Points

Completing asynchronous coursework, even when facilitated, can be an overwhelming undertaking for an online learner. The high drop-out rates for many online programs help illustrate this. Many people have a difficult time juggling their professional and personal lives with the completion of their online academic responsibilities. It can be difficult to set aside time and stay on task to complete coursework independently. Even highly motivated learners may struggle to structure their time to stay on top of their studies. For some learners, synchronous sessions provide an answer. They serve as anchor points—discrete time-based milestones that can be entered into their personal calendars and actually achieved. Attendance at these events can then serve to motivate learners, re-affirm their confidence and will, and provide enough momentum to propel them to the next live anchor point while they accomplish their independent or asynchronous work along the way.

Just-in-Time Assistance

The live online availability of an instructor, peer, advisor, tutor, or reference librarian means that learners can find reinforcements to *keep* them on task even when they *are* on task. Live online chat support offered on a library's Web site or live tutors made available via virtual meeting rooms, for example, can provide the just-in-time assistance a learner needs to stay engaged with a given assignment and not give up out of frustration or a sense of isolation. Anytime-anywhere online learning programs are really all-the-time enterprises today, and institutions are beginning to address the need for access to live academic, technical, advising, or peer support at virtually any time as well.

Combine self-directed, meaningful, active assignments within an online course with the availability of a live online instructor willing to help you stay on task and walk you through things, and you have the makings of some pretty powerful learning moments. In this example, Paul Stacey of BCcampus describes his involvement from the student perspective in a virtual lab component of one of Ron Evan's astronomy courses:

> At 11:00 at night I found myself online "live" in a virtual meeting room working with Ron Evans who teaches two online astronomy courses at North Island College in British Columbia, Canada. The astronomy courses have a virtual lab component that makes use of an online observatory Ron set up in a small domed building at remote Tatla Lake where the night time sky is free of city light pollution. The observatory has a fourteen inch telescope and high resolution digital camera connected to the Internet. Students dispersed all over the province use the Web to control the telescope and take pictures of stars and planets which they can download to their computer and incorporate in lab reports. Students conducting their virtual lab assignments can meet Ron in a live chat room or audio-enabled virtual meeting room where he is available to guide them through the task.
>
> On this night Ron and I worked together live online for a demonstration of how students use the live online telescope. Ron used application sharing to show me how to use the Web interface that controls the

telescope and allows students to download pictures to their computers. We lucked out with good weather and a cloud free night time sky. Dialoguing live online I followed Ron's audio instructions and using the software specified which planet I wished to photograph. I set the shutter speed and snapped pictures! The live nature of the session allowed us to examine each picture right on the spot. We took a number of pictures of several different planets together, and then I continued to shoot a few more on my own, just as Ron's students do. (Stacey, personal communication, June 5, 2005)

Live online, accessible, just-in-time support like this—to make no mention of engaging activities—gives learners little excuse or opportunity to drop the ball and abandon the task.

HIGH EXPECTATIONS

> *Good practice communicates high expectations.*
>
> —A. Chickering and Z. Gamson (1987)

When my first-grade teacher Eleanor Sachs gave me half of her tuna sandwich on the first day of school (because I had forgotten my lunchbox at home), she humanized herself by coming to her student's aid, and set herself up in my young mind as someone I would never disappoint. We can probably all think of people from our own learning experiences that somehow managed to make us feel as though letting them down would be letting ourselves down. This feeling can translate into higher motivation and better performance.

Sometimes expectations are set implicitly by virtue of *how* teacher-student interaction unfolds, as in the case of Mrs. Sachs and her student; other times they are conveyed quite specifically by *what* an instructor says. Either way, we know that communicating high expectations of students helps them succeed. The synchronous environment is well equipped for communicating expectations, directly, clearly, and with humanity.

A Human Environment

Real-time online venues help instructors and learners in completely online situations perceive each other more as the human beings they actually are than their disembodied names and textual contributions would otherwise convey. The more we understand the nature and personality of a learner—and the more the learner respects us as humans concerned about their success—the more likely appropriate expectations can be set and met. Citing Pratt's earlier work on "the electronic personality," Palloff and Pratt enumerate several elements that help personality take shape online. Among them are

- The ability to create a mental picture of the partner in the communication process
- The ability to create a sense of presence online through the personalization of communications (Palloff and Pratt, 1999, p. 22)

Synchronous settings can do better than create a "sense of presence"; they can actually permit presence itself. And with presence comes a less encumbered way to convey ideas, emotion, sense of humor, and expectations. The ability to use voice in real time to communicate with others online is arguably more than a small step in humanizing a course; it is a huge leap. Add video to the equation when it is feasible, and you can do far more than create "a mental picture" of instructor and peers. All of this translates into an environment in which expectations are transmitted through faces, mouths, voices, and sometimes even eyes, all of which are far harder to ignore than those seemingly coming from a computer alone.

The synchronous environment also allows us to better individualize the expectations we have for each learner in our courses. Interacting with students in real time makes them more "three dimensional" and offers insights into their capabilities, inhibitions, and motivations. It helps instructors to better set and convey the bar of expectations for each student, and to do so in a manner that motivates.

Clearer Expectations and More Ways to Achieve Them

When instructors communicate assignments and expectations in synchronous venues, they have the opportunity to immediately gauge whether learners understand or accept them. Learners can ask for clarification or for more explicit instruction before heading off to do a task, thereby reducing the risk of situations where conveying direction by text alone results in misunderstandings. In fact, when instructors interact with learners live online, expectations and instructions can even be efficiently generated through real-time collaboration with students

(Chickering and Ehrmann, 1996), thus giving them a greater stake in the process and the outcome.

Furthermore, providing opportunities for learners to meet expectations by using synchronous tools, as well as asynchronous ones, opens up a whole new palette of expressive and creative options for students and a vast new array of means by which to assess them. Live student-led lessons based on their research, online gallery talks through their e-portfolios, and voice-based debates demonstrating their newfound comfort with a topic all are possible when instructors allow their expectations to flow out horizontally across the many communication modes now available.

DIVERSE TALENTS AND WAYS OF LEARNING

Good practice respects diverse talents and ways of learning.

—A. Chickering and Z. Gamson (1987)

The world in which we all live and work is both synchronous and asynchronous. When a supervisor calls us on the phone, we are in a synchronous communications mode. When we write a report or book, we are in an asynchronous mode. When the doorbell rings and we answer it, when we go into a meeting, or when we show up for a job interview our real-time communication skills are called into gear. When we compose a letter to our elected officials, leave a voice mail message for a colleague, send an e-mail requesting support to a software company, or leave a sticky note on someone's computer, we tap into our asynchronous communication abilities. Some of us are more comfortable with some of the above scenarios than others, as different people do indeed have diverse talents and ways of learning.

Many face-to-face instructors will cross paths with students who they just know will be quite successful in their careers but not necessarily because of the grades they get in class; they know this from how the learners carry themselves and how they interact with others. Some will describe these people by saying things such as, "He has a way with people," or "She has a commanding presence." In online courses, outside of synchronous venues, these kinds of student strengths are more difficult, if not impossible, to recognize and therefore harder to tap into when encouraging students to express themselves and succeed.

Until recently, asynchronous communication has been favored predominantly over real-time means of interaction. The most common rationale offered for dismissing the potential of synchronous venues is that learning online is primarily motivated by convenience and programs that have time-based components are inherently inconvenient. (See, for example, an online discussion from The Distance Education Online Symposium ["Time Spent During Synchronous Meetings?" DEOS-L, 2005] in which this common debate played out.) Yet the ability for synchronous communication to enhance the overall quality of online learning, increase interaction, and offer opportunities to tap into a greater number of learning and teaching styles has been given much more attention. Haefner writes: "It is hard to imagine teaching without both [asynchronous and synchronous] modes of interacting with our students, and I can't believe many teachers would want to handicap their teaching by relying on just one of them" (2000). Coghlan advances the idea in suggesting: "Some learners need the more human contact that synchronous and particularly voice events provide, and the more attuned a student is to the learning environment, and to the people they share that environment with, the more likely it is that effective learning will occur" (2004b, p. 7).

Even within a real-time venue, there are often multiple channels through which learners and instructors can choose to interact. Some may find safety in text communication; others may prefer the naturalness and ease of voice. In multichanneled environments such as virtual classrooms or virtual meeting rooms, facilitators may find that given a choice, certain individuals or entire groups will opt for one method over another. There are times to coddle these preferences and times to force people out of their comfort zone so that they may learn a new skill.

The use of synchronous tools to offer learners options to fit their communication preferences also extends to face-to-face learning. In this example, Buthaina Al Othman describes an activity she crafted for an "English for Science" course taught at Kuwait University:

> Many of my students have good speaking and listening skills acquired from watching American-English movies. However, most of them lacked independent and critical thinking skills and the ability to deal with impromptu situations. To develop these skills I designed a final project for this class that required students to write and present term papers either in the face-to-face classroom or live online; it was their choice. Some preferred presenting in a room where they could see their audience, while others opted for the safety of being at the keyboard. I

organized multiple venue presentations, delivered before a global audience composed of a remote group of ESL/EFL [English as a second language, English as a foreign language] teachers from Denmark, Spain, Australia, Saudi Arabia, Portugal, Germany, Greece, and Brazil, and a local group of thirteen students, physically attending at the Kuwait University Distance Learning Center.

We used a virtual classroom that supported text and voice and had a facility to project PowerPoint or Web pages. The project created constructive academic competition among students, resulting in very good oral presentations. All spoke good English in loud, clear voices and maintained good eye contact. When they were not sure how to respond, they used professional expressions, such as "I'm sorry I don't know the answer" and "I promise to further research the point and bring you the answer as soon as I can."

The online and face-to-face presentations positively influenced the class, enhancing various language, computer, and Internet skills. My students were motivated to continue their learning; one of them was interested in taking an elective advanced English for Science critique writing course to improve her writing with critical thinking. Others requested information about sites offering online English courses to improve their English.

This activity encouraged students to look for new ways to improve their learning and studying strategies, which means they were taking the first step toward independent learning, an essential approach toward learning in the twenty-first century. (Al Othman, personal communication, 2005)

As the success of Al Othman's activity demonstrates, this seventh principle of good practice applies to computer-mediated environments that Chickering and Gamson could probably not have imagined when they summarized years of research and experience. No matter where our students learn, they do need opportunities to showcase who they are and what they can do while also pushing their own limits to learn and perform in new ways.

Tools for Learning in Real Time

T he sheer number of real-time options and the ever-expanding vocabulary associated with these tools can be overwhelming. As with any instructional design scenario, it is often best to work backwards from the learning goals at hand to the identification of tools and features that will best make those goals achievable. To that end, it is instructive to have a good sense as to what tools are in the toolbox as one sets out to craft the best possible experience to address a set of learning objectives.

This chapter considers some of the more common varieties of synchronous tools. In making sense of the synchronous landscape, there is more than one way to categorize the many real-time features available. Thanks to digital convergence— the ongoing fusing of tools from previously distinct realms of communication—the categories are bound to blur over time. Nonetheless, I have tried to group tools described here according to whether they involve live text, live audio and video, or the display of visuals that enrich learning or collaboration. I have also included descriptions of some of the tools that help manage synchronous environments from a more administrative or logistical perspective. For hands-on examples of these and the latest real-time tools in action, you are encouraged to visit this book's companion Web site, www.learninginrealtime.com.

Chapter Four will assemble these tools into their most common configurations or "venues" and look more closely at how they are put to use in actual learning situations.

TEXT-BASED TOOLS

One of the most basic synchronous features is *text messaging* or *chat,* which involves the exchange of instantaneous text-based messages between two or more people in real time. An assumption with text messaging is that the intended audience for these messages is present at the current moment, albeit virtually, and able to receive them and respond immediately, thus forming a real-time online dialogue. This expectation of "presence" is what differentiates chat from an asynchronous form of communication such as e-mail or discussion boards.

Presence Indicators. Text messaging tools usually provide some kind of *presence indicator,* a list of real names, nicknames, or user names of those participating. The list dynamically updates itself to reflect current participation as people enter and leave a conversation.

Chat Logs or Transcripts. A chat log is a transcript or record of a text-based chat session. Sometimes these logs are created and made available automatically for viewing by the chat software being used, and in other instances an individual participant needs to save the transcript on his or her own. Chat transcripts will often include time stamps for each message so that one can sense the pace of the conversation when reading it after the fact.

Private or Instant Messaging. It is not uncommon to have the ability to direct a message or carry on a private conversation with a selected individual. This private messaging can also be called *instant messaging* or IM.

Moderated Chat. Some tools allow designated moderators to screen messages before permitting them to be viewed by all members of a group. This feature is usually meant for use with very large, live online events, including those open to the public. A moderated chat function can also aid in facilitating activities in creative ways with smaller numbers of learners. For example, an instructor might ask a question and initially withhold all responses, releasing just specific comments into public view to stimulate group discussion in the manner or order desired.

Avatars. Some real-time text messaging tools allow participants to import or select from a library of icons, images, photos, or characters to represent themselves on screen. These *avatars* are meant to convey a sense of the personality, individuality, or current mood of each person involved.

Entry and Exit Announcements. Text-based environments often display messages that announce the arrival or departure of participants. Together with a participant list, these announcements—such as "Amelia Earhart has entered the room" or "Albert Einstein has exited the room"—can help direct each user's attention to the changing composition of the group. Text-based entry and exit announcements can be handy when reviewing chat transcripts, as they complete the picture as to who was present during specific segments of an online activity.

Action Messages. Some tools provide icons or text commands that express physical movement through *action messages*. For example, in some systems, such as Internet Relay Chat (IRC), one might type

/me stomps his feet

This command would show up for other participants in the chat dialogue as

*Jonathan stomps his feet

Action messages can also be expressed in some tools by selecting from a library of icons or animated images, such as a cartoon of someone waving, laughing, winking, or blushing.

Sound Effects. Auditory signals, such as canned applause or a virtual knock on the door, are present in some chat systems. These can be useful for participants who are multitasking and not looking directly at their chat interface; sound indicators can help them keep up with an unfolding dialogue. For some, sounds can become a nuisance, but most sound control features can be disabled and enabled by each individual.

Text Formatting. Some tools make it possible to format the size, font, style, and color of the messages sent or received. Formatting serves a variety of purposes, including improving visibility, placing emphasis on certain words or messages, or expressing individuality. Formatting options sometimes allow a participant to "tag" certain users such that messages sent from them show up in a different color, thus making it easier to isolate certain trains of thought.

LIVE AUDIO AND VIDEO TOOLS

We turn our attention now to an exploration of tools that enable real-time audio and video communication online. These tools furnish a familiar environment for the kind of natural give and take characteristic of in-person human exchanges.

Live Audio

In thinking about the transmission of live audio on the Web, it is worth noting that the introduction of Alexander Graham Bell's telephone—which he initially called the "harmonic telegraph"—was greeted in 1876 with sheer wonderment. Showcased for the first time in public at the Philadelphia Centennial before a panel that included the Emperor of Brazil, the telephone caused a great commotion. According to Bell's biographer, the Emperor tried it, stood up promptly, and shouted: "I hear, I hear!" (Bruce, 1973, p. 197). Smithsonian Institution curator Barney Finn put the excitement into context: "This was a rather startling thing, after all: to be able to talk into one thing, and then hundreds of feet away, you hear something at the receiver" (WGBH, 1997).

Even though the excitement of hearing live voice communication over a computer may not cause the same degree of elation that the telephone did, there is still something many find unforgettable about the first time someone speaks directly to them from the computer on their desk. Perhaps, as with the first telephone, it is the sense of disembodiment of the voice from the person speaking, and the momentary sense that it is the computer itself—and not a human—that is doing the talking that causes the double-take. Nonetheless, once the novelty wears off, what remains is a powerful and versatile tool for learning live online.

I will talk about specific ways to facilitate and utilize real-time voice communication in online learning settings in the next chapters, but first let us look at some of the specific characteristics of real-time, audio-based tools available on the Web.

Voice over IP. The transmission of voice over the Internet is commonly called Voice over Internet Protocol or VoIP, and it travels over the same kinds of networks that carry other Internet data, such as Web pages or e-mail. This is unique from traditional telephone voice transmission, which historically has used dedicated circuit-based voice transmission lines. One of the advantages in educational and collaborative situations of VoIP-based audio is that there is a wide and growing array of ways to use Web-based interfaces to control and orchestrate audio-based exchanges. The result can be innovative and engaging ways to facilitate live one-on-one and group learning activities and conversations among people in different geographical locations.

Broadcast. One form of receiving live audio on the Internet is in a broadcast mode, whereby audio is heard by a group of people connecting to a central computer or server that is distributing the feed. Often referred to as a *Webcast,* this form of communicating live on the Web is *simplex* in nature, meaning that audio is only transmitted in one direction. Although other tools can be used in conjunction with Webcast audio to allow real-time or near real-time communication from listeners back to the leaders of the event, by its nature broadcasting alone is a one-way channel of communication.

One common form of Webcasting is called *streaming,* which is the process by which audio information is sent over the Internet in a succession of small units called packets, and then heard by the listener as each of those packets is received. Streaming is usually characterized by some degree of latency or delay, such that listeners may be hearing a person's audio several seconds after her words were originally spoken. One of the reasons for this delay is a process called *buffering* whereby the tool receiving the audio over the Internet stores several seconds of audio before it begins to play. This reserve or buffer of audio is drawn upon if the live transmission is ever delayed as it travels over the Internet. Although buffering can improve the quality of audio that is heard, the latency does make real-time feed-back from listeners somewhat challenging to accommodate.

Half Duplex. When a tool allows two-way voice interaction but with only one person allowed to speak at a time, that tool is called *half duplex*. Such tools use only one audio channel, so while that channel is in use to transmit the voice of one person, other people cannot be heard. For those familiar with walkie-talkies, the effect is quite similar.

Most half-duplex audio systems are less demanding on bandwidth. This can help ensure that learners with slower connection to the Internet can participate more readily. Half-duplex audio arguably keeps conversations quite orderly, almost parliamentary, in nature, with only one individual identified to speak at a given moment. For requiring the immediacy of telephone or face-to-face dialogue, half-duplex tools may feel somewhat unnatural, although most people will get acclimated with use.

Full Duplex. Synchronous audio tools that are *full duplex* allow audio to flow in both directions at one time, and therefore allow two or more people to converse online in much the same manner as a telephone or conference call.

Audio Controls. Some real-time audio controls allow instructors to determine who in a group is permitted to speak, and who is muted at any given time. A queuing feature is not uncommon and allows people to indicate their desire to speak. Such controls become very important in real-time environments with large groups of learners. If too many are allowed to speak at once, it can be difficult to hear and can possibly inundate available bandwidth.

Telephony Integration. What used to be disparate ways of carrying on real-time audio conversations have converged within many live online audio tools. Telephone integration with VoIP tools increases the flexibility for learners in how they can participate in real-time online activities. Some tools allow participants to use standard telephone calls to join classmates in VoIP-based conversations. A number of synchronous venues exclusively use the telephone in conjunction with a Web-based visual interface and dispense with VoIP entirely. Such systems often have Web-based methods for controlling voice participation by standard telephone during online sessions. For example, an instructor can use on-screen buttons to dial out and connect students by telephone, or selectively mute specific participants' phones.

Live Video

Live online video tools have been available for some time and are continually getting better and more reliable. Quality, real-time online video, perhaps more than most other tools, relies on a dependable, broadband Internet connection. Although in some instances video can be feasible at lower bandwidth connections with smaller image sizes and reduced image quality, it is still quite susceptible to delays in transmission and Internet traffic. Nonetheless, technical barriers are diminishing rapidly with the number of broadband connections rising, and multiway, live online video is becoming more of a reality.

To some extent, the availability of live online video helps level the playing field between offline and online learning venues by offering the ability to capture and share the subtleties of facial expressions and movement. Implemented creatively and intelligently, live video tools have an important role to play in a wide range of real-time online learning scenarios. However, live online video also offers the easiest path to preserve the status quo way of doing things, such as enshrining lecturing online as the same fixture it has been in campus-based environments.

Carol Twigg is among those who caution us against taking this path. "The problem with applying old solutions to new problems in the world of online learning," she says, "is that these applications tend to produce results that are 'as good as' what we have done before" (2001, p. 4). Twigg is referring to the so-called "no significant difference" (Russell, 2002) phenomenon, whereby numerous studies have found that online courses can be as effective as their offline equivalents. Twigg instructively continues: "These studies have typically been used by distance educators to defend the quality of their courses and programs against the once-predominant view that learning takes place only in a physical classroom. What we need now, however, are new approaches that go beyond producing no significant difference" (p. 4). Chapters Five and Six will look at some of these approaches to facilitating learning activities in real-time online environments, both with and without video.

Live Video Display. When only one person is transmitting live video during a session, the user interface involved is usually quite straightforward. If two or more people broadcast live video at the same time, a variety of possibilities arises for displaying the concurrent feeds.

Some tools indicate with an icon those participants who are sending video and allow others to click to view them. Another approach involves *voice activation,* whereby a participant's video automatically appears on screen when the system detects them speaking. A basic *split screen* allows two people—such as the instructor and one learner—to be seen side by side at the same time. Some systems will also use *tiling* or *thumbnails* to present a smaller or periodic still-frame capture of each participant so that instructors or learners can "see" everyone at once. This is what I call the *Brady Bunch Effect* (a reference to the pop American television program that began with the screen split nine ways to show all members of the title family at one time).

The most advanced live online video systems allow a tremendous amount of customization to the interface. Video windows can be dynamically resized and moved around the screen in real-time, and the number of people who can be seen at once can be adjusted.

Bandwidth Detection and Video Quality. A variety of factors affect the quality of video transmitted over the Web, including

- Amount of available bandwidth to send and receive video stream
- Number of video frames per second
- Dimensions (height and width) of the video image
- Number of colors used or whether color is used at all
- Codec, or encoding protocol, used to compress the video for transmission

Some tools automatically adjust these settings by detecting what a particular person's Internet connection or computer can handle. Others rely on participants or instructors to make adjustments accordingly.

CONTENT, DISPLAY, AND OTHER INTERACTIVE TOOLS

Thus far we have focused upon channels for text, audio, and video communication. We will now survey tools for the shared viewing of visual and other interactive content within real-time environments.

Virtual Whiteboard

Virtual whiteboards allow for impromptu drawing and annotation on a shared virtual surface. The most basic whiteboards offer a facilitator or participant the ability to use digital drawing tools to create free-form lines, ovals, squares, or text in various colors, shapes, and sizes that are seen by all present in the virtual venue at the same time.

Moderated Use and Accountability. The more robust whiteboard tools allow all participants to annotate the screen at one time or for select participants to be granted permission by a facilitator. Some tools will display what contributions to a collective drawing were made by which participant. This option can be useful in ensuring a level of accountability for virtual whiteboard markings.

Image Imports and Layers. Many whiteboards allow participants to import images and manipulate multiple layers of graphics or annotations. An image import function enables learners to share their own work with others in real time and receive immediate feedback. In addition to showing digital photographs or other images, some tools allow one to take a screen capture or copy anything displayed on one's computer screen—such as an essay, spreadsheet, or Web page—and add it to the virtual whiteboard for others to see. Whiteboard drawing tools are often layered over other visuals, such as class slides or diagrams, and are used by instructors or students to draw emphasis, solve problems, clarify complexity, invite spontaneity, take notes, or conduct other dynamic activities. Figure 3.1 provides an illustration of how participants might use a shared whiteboard in a real-time, online psychology class to visually enlighten a discussion on the relationship between certain personality attributes.

Object-oriented. Virtual whiteboards that are *object-oriented* provide the most flexibility in how the tool can be used to facilitate learning. Each mark, line, or item placed on an object-oriented whiteboard can later be moved around the screen, copied, pasted, or adjusted in color, size, or shape. Examples of creative uses of a digital object-oriented whiteboard are offered in Chapter Six on designing real-time activities.

Application Sharing or Screen Sharing

An application-sharing tool allows instructors and learners to show programs running on their computer to others in the same real-time session. For example, an

Figure 3.1. Sample Whiteboard Screen Displaying Impromptu Learning Activity in a Live Online Psychology Class.

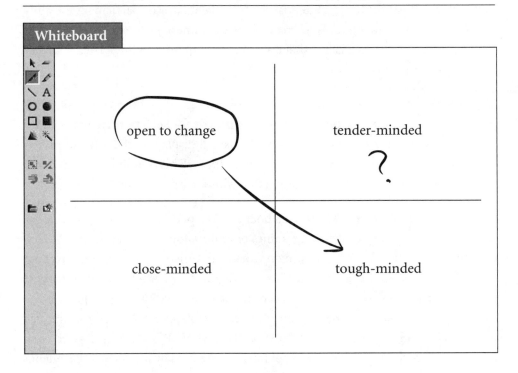

instructor might open up a favorite word processing application and broadcast a document—a student paper, for example—to learners in the live online class. Most application-sharing tools will broadcast the mouse movements and follow all of the navigational steps taken by the person sharing their screen.

True application sharing allows just that—sharing. A person who is broadcasting a program for others to see can select a user to "share" or take control of the application. Once control is "passed," selected users can control the mouse movement and application on the remote computer. In this manner, knowledge or comprehension can be demonstrated by learners, or the person whose computer is being shown can seek assistance or invite collaboration.

File Transfer

With application-sharing tools, the file or document shown is rarely sent to participants; instead, an image of it is "projected" for others to see. Some tools, however, do permit the real-time transfer of files from one computer to another within a live session. These file-sharing tools circumvent the need to e-mail a file attachment or upload a document to a course Web site.

Slide Showing

Many synchronous online venues feature the ability for instructors to show or guide participants through a set of slides or other visual aids, a practice akin to the projection of overheads or slides on a screen in a physical classroom. Most tools with this feature allow the facilitator to "push" the desired slide to all participants at the same time, thus controlling what they see on their screen at any given moment.

Background Loading. Many systems that include slide-showing functionality use protocols to optimize the transfer of slides to participants. During real-time sessions, it can be disconcerting to participants if they must wait for the appearance of visuals being referenced at a particular moment. Well-designed tools will transfer slides in the background so that they will be ready to appear instantaneously when called up by a facilitator.

Preservation of Special Effects. Some slide-showing tools will preserve the special effects or animations created in a slide-authoring program when showing those visuals to participants online in real time. Others will ignore ancillary information such as motion, hyperlinks, and slide notes and just provide a static image for each slide.

Slide Libraries. It is not uncommon to be able to store and categorize visual content online for future or ongoing use. With an online slide library in place, one can login from any computer and easily call up a set of lesson materials. This sense of "persistence" of content allows for on-the-fly adaptation to learner needs or questions during real-time events. Everything is at one's fingertips. The more advanced slide or content libraries allow users to decide whether some of their materials can be shared with others on the system, thereby essentially creating a communal repository. As standards take root and communities of practice continue to grow in the realm of real-time online learning tools, it will become increasingly easy for instructors to import virtual slide "decks" or "carousels" from publicly accessible global storehouses of real-time visual aids.

Course Map or Site Map Integration

Some online course sites or learning management systems—like many Web sites in general—have convenient *site maps* or outline views of all of the sections, pages, content, or documents found in a given site. One clever way to leverage the asynchronous content already available in an online course site is to be able to view this site or course map from within a real-time environment and "push" out specific items live during a real-time session. Such tools provide an easy way to weave asynchronous activities and resources into synchronous experiences.

Web Tours

When in a real-time learning venue, the entire World Wide Web is one's "slide tray." Any page on the Internet can be brought up for all participants to see and peruse at the same time to achieve any number of instructional purposes. Whether one is improving the authenticity of a learning experience through joint exploration of primary source materials, up-to-the-minute data, or breaking news, the combination of live Web pages and the real-time presence of learners is very powerful.

Guided Web Tours. Referred to by some as "follow-me browsing" or "Web safari," guided Web tour tools allow one to click from site to site on the Web with other live participants in tow. Many systems will allow those "following the leader" to meander off to explore independently by using hyperlinks on a given page. At the leader's discretion, all participants can be synchronized with one another, ending any individual excursions.

Clickable Hyperlinks. Most synchronous Web-based venues will automatically convert typed Web addresses into hyperlinks, which can be clicked and visited at the discretion of participants. This saves the need to copy, paste, or retype resources shared during the flow of an event.

Previewing and Filtering. Web pages are dynamic resources, and their contents can change at any time. When one brings learners to a Web page in real time, it is possible for the unpredictable to happen: what was on a Web page visited just yesterday is no longer there today, or worse, has been replaced by something not appropriate for a class activity. A "preview" mode allows facilitators to preview and approve all Web pages before they are brought up on participant computers.

Polling and Quizzing

As we have discussed, immediacy and granularity of feedback are among the great benefits of live online learning environments. Instantaneous measures of learner understanding permit a lesson plan to be adjusted on the fly and remediation to be offered at the exact moment of need. One genre of tool that permits a quick read of learner status is polling or quizzing functions embedded directly into a synchronous platform.

Question Types. Synchronous polling tools often include single answer, multiple answer, and free-form response options. In many cases, the instructor can peruse results privately in real time and choose to publish results for all to see. A handful of real-time polling tools will allow select answers to be showcased to the group and permit the instructor to publicly hone in on a response of particular interest. A few product developers have created database-driven tools enabling live online matching, brainstorming, and ranking exercises with feedback collected going to an instructor or the full group.

Display of Results. Polling results can be displayed numerically, in lists, or in graphical formats. Most polling and quizzing tools provide real-time, dynamically updated pie charts, bar graphs, and histograms that change before one's eyes as individuals submit responses. Both anonymous and non-anonymous poll types are usually available.

Online Course Integration. In some cases, the integration between synchronous tools and course Web sites are advanced enough to allow a quiz or survey authored within an online course management platform to be administered live to students within the real-time online venue. It is advisable to think carefully before turning the live online environment into a testing room. This approach will rarely honor the "synchronous compact" discussed in Chapter One. Quizzes and surveys employed during a live session should be brief and should advance the cause of the immediate learning objectives at hand for a given live session. Otherwise, they should be deployed as independent activities before or after the synchronous experience.

Activity Indicators and Remote Screen Viewing

Real-time environments often feature nonverbal indicators depicting the current online activity of others. These visuals help bring meaning to moments of "silence" during live online exchanges. One of the most common indicators shows when a remote participant is in the process of typing a text-based comment. This might be represented through an icon that lights up, or it can appear as a discrete momentary message, such as *Dale is typing*. Sometimes indicators also show *inactivity* by displaying messages like *Michelle is idle* or *Michelle is away* when a participant does not interact with the system for a given period of time or voluntarily decides to indicate that she has stepped away from her computer for a moment.

Some tools are capable of transmitting information to an instructor about whether a learner has "minimized" the synchronous interface and is using another application. An extension of this is "remote desktop viewing" functionality, which allows an instructor—either via a thumbnail or a full-screen view—to essentially look "over the shoulder" and see what any given participant is doing on his or her computer.

Multimedia

The richness of real-time human interaction can be compounded in the presence of rich media content. Vibrant Web resources—such as animations, video clips, interactive diagrams, or authentic audio sound bites—when experienced alone can be captivating casting off points for independent learning. Add to them the real-time presence of an expert or of a group of peers ready to explore, and one has the recipe for some learning adventures.

Web-based synchronous platforms have a wide range of tools to support multimedia integration into the live experience. At the simplest level, one can "point" to a media-rich resource that exists on a Web site during a real-time session. More sophisticated real-time platforms have tools for storing and playing various media objects right from within the application. The Web houses ever-growing repositories of video clips, audio recordings, podcasts, interactive exhibits, animations, and other media, and many instructors today have access to people with skills to create original multimedia content. The possibilities are endless when it comes to bringing these elements into a real-time session.

Breakout Rooms

In physical venues, it is not uncommon for an instructor to want to divide a room of learners into smaller groups to work on team projects, discuss a particular issue, or receive specialized guidance in a more intimate setting. Breakout rooms like this are possible in the virtual world as well. Tools that allow the subdivision of virtual space are available in text-based venues as well as more media-rich ones that include audio and video. Some tools allow "rooms" to be created on the fly; others require some forethought as to how many spaces will be needed. The more complete tools permit a lead instructor to designate moderators for each room who are given extra sets of privileges to manage the smaller groups.

Recording and Playback

I have already mentioned text messaging transcripts or chat logs as a way of saving a record of an online text-based exchange. Tools that incorporate live audio and video often also have a recording function, which can be of enormous value in reaping the same kind of time-shifting benefits that are the hallmarks of asynchronous interaction. With a recording function, a live event can be played back at any time. It offers a just-in-time resource for all learners to review, whether they attended the original live session or not.

Navigation and Searching. The most thoughtfully designed tools for playing back recorded live online learning activities include the ability to easily navigate and pinpoint moments of particular interest. One method involves an automatically generated, clickable index based on Web pages shown, text comments typed, or slides displayed. There are synchronous platforms that integrate automatically digitized handwritten notes taken by each student in such a way that a learner can click on his or her own comments and be brought to the moment in the live class session when those notes were jotted down.

Feedback. Although recordings are often posted in a course Web site where learners can make use of tools such as discussion boards to continue dialogues started during live sessions, a *feedback* option is sometimes available from within a recording. This option allows a learner to send a message to an instructor if questions arise during playback.

Availability. Depending on the nature of the tool being used, recordings can be made that reside on an individual participant's computer or that are only available by linking to a server or Web site for playback from a central location. Local recordings can be played back at any time without an Internet connection. With centrally stored recordings, access can more easily be controlled, and content updates can be made without an impractical recall.

Editing. With the increasing use of real-time learning environments, more people want the ability to edit recordings of their live sessions. Tools in this arena are developing that emulate other software for postproduction work, such as those used for digital movies and sound editing.

Automatic Technical Checks

Many synchronous venues include Web-based tools that are accessed in advance of a live session to simulate the technical demands that will be placed on a learner's computer during the actual event. They indicate whether the computer meets the requirement to participate and offer specific troubleshooting guidance when it does not.

Three-Dimensional Rendering of Space and People

Some virtual environments allow participants to choose landscapes, plan cities, design floor plans, take on desired body types, and don virtual outfits and hair styles to represent themselves visually online. These multi-user virtual environments, or MUVEs, provide learners with the added dimensions of place, movement, and "physicality" when interacting with peers and instructors online.

Specialized Tools and Templates

One of the most fertile areas for synchronous learning tool development is in the creation of specialized, discipline-specific templates and features for use within real-time online classes or meetings.

Imagine a chemistry teacher entering a synchronous environment and finding a virtual "lab table" replete with three-dimensional renditions of Bunsen burners and flasks filled with chemicals, and a remotely assembled group of actual learners awaiting guidance on how to conduct their online experiments. Think about an architecture professor equipped in a live online "studio" with a set of specialized computer-aided design tools for coaching students on their renderings, or a civics teacher presiding over a class debate in which all synchronous online interactions were automatically governed by *Robert's Rules of Order*. A growing number of these kinds of simulations and tools exist today, but relatively few of them are built specifically for real-time online environments. As synchronous venues find their place in the online learning landscape, creative instructors will provide the impetus for a vast specialization of the toolsets available in live online venues to meet the needs of learners in all disciplines. It is an exciting prospect.

Real-Time Learning Venues

D ifferent kinds of learning activities call for different kinds of learning venues. Rooms on a physical academic campus, for example, come in different sizes and configurations and are equipped with different resources. Some are publicly available spaces, and others are reserved for use by special groups. A professor might use a large lecture hall with a projection screen for full-class gatherings, but a teaching assistant will request a small seminar room with a round table for class discussion. A group of students working on a team project might find a quiet alcove in the library with a whiteboard, while another student steps up to a reference desk for a one-on-one conversation with a librarian. And a handful of students might visit a professor in her office to clarify a concept, while others do chemistry experiments or write computer code in a lab. We must not forget the group of extended family members and friends who watch commencement activities on a large screen for overflow crowds not lucky enough to secure seats in the main graduation arena.

We choose different kinds of spaces to assemble with others because each offers a unique set of needed resources and a "feel" that seems right for the gathering at hand. The same is true online. Web-based venues come in many configurations, with unique sets of tools to accommodate groups of different sizes and for various purposes.

A MOVING TARGET

Trying to define and describe every type of online venue that currently exists for real-time teaching and learning, however, is like shooting a moving target. Although offline we may all have a relatively similar conception as to what constitutes a classroom, each instructor and software provider has his or her own idea as to what defines a virtual classroom. Some consider a text messaging tool with a slide-showing utility a *virtual classroom,* while others call those combined components a *chat room,* and reserve *virtual classroom* for a platform that includes live audio or video. Furthermore, the various components comprised in each type of venue—the tools described in the last section—can, in effect, appear in an infinite number of combinations and permutations. Table 4.1 attempts to capture this moving target and offer a snapshot of features found in various venues. As technologies improve, many of these real-time tools are converging, and venues are more likely to be differentiated by other factors, such as specialization of their toolsets for specific disciplines; interoperability on all kinds of devices, like computers, mobile PDAs (personal digital assistants), and phones; and integration with leading course management systems and operating systems. Just as there are many styles of mobile phones, cars, and physical classrooms to meet different needs, so, too, is there a wide selection of real-time online communication tools for different situations (Figure 4.1). No one platform is likely to ever do it all.

That said, a brief description of some of the more common venues referenced today—and the kinds of tools that most often characterize them—is very useful for our conversation here. If we are to consider practical teaching and learning strategies, which we will do in Chapters Five and Six, a common vocabulary is practical.

CHAT ROOMS

A chat room is typically a text-based venue where groups of participants exchange typed messages in real time. Chat rooms can sometimes include visual tools, such

Table 4.1. Features Found in Synchronous Online Venues: A Snapshot of a Moving Target.

Legend:
- ● Frequently or always
- ◐ Sometimes
- ○ Rarely or never

Features	Instant Messaging (IM)	Chat Room	MUVE	Virtual Reference Desk	Virtual Office/Meeting Room	Virtual Classroom	Interactive Webcasting	Webcasting	In-Class Online Aids
Up to two people	●	○	○	●	●	○	○	○	○
Small Groups	◐	●	●	◐	●	◐	◐	○	●
Medium–Large groups	○	●	●	○	○	◐	●	●	○
Text messaging	●	●	●	●	●	●	●	◐	◐
Avatars	◐	◐	●	◐	◐	◐	○	○	◐
Emoticons	●	●	●	●	●	●	●	○	○
Activity Indicators	●	●	◐	◐	◐	◐	◐	○	◐
Live One-Way Audio	◐	○	○	◐	◐	◐	◐	●	◐
Live Two-Way Audio	◐	○	○	◐	◐	◐	◐	○	◐
Live One-Way Video	◐	○	○	◐	◐	◐	◐	◐	◐
Live Two-Way Video	◐	○	○	◐	◐	◐	◐	○	◐
Shared Virtual Whiteboard	◐	◐	○	◐	●	●	●	○	◐
Slide Showing	○	◐	◐	◐	◐	●	●	◐	●
Authoring Area	○	○	◐	◐	◐	◐	◐	◐	◐
Site Map Integration	○	◐	○	◐	◐	◐	○	○	●
Application Sharing	◐	○	○	◐	●	●	◐	◐	◐
File Transfer	●	◐	◐	◐	◐	◐	◐	○	●
Web Tours	◐	◐	◐	●	●	●	●	◐	●
Polling	○	◐	◐	◐	◐	●	◐	○	●
Quizzing	○	○	○	●	◐	●	◐	◐	●
Multimedia Playback	○	○	○	◐	◐	●	◐	◐	●
Remote Screen Viewing	◐	○	◐	◐	◐	◐	○	○	●
Messaging Transcripts	◐	●	◐	●	◐	●	◐	○	●
Recording	○	○	◐	◐	◐	●	●	●	●
Playback	○	○	◐	◐	◐	●	●	●	●
Breakout Rooms	○	●	●	◐	◐	◐	◐	○	◐
3-D Rendering	○	◐	●	◐	○	○	○	○	○
Specialized Templates	○	○	◐	◐	◐	◐	◐	◐	◐

Figure 4.1. Uses for Real-Time Online Venues.

Venue	Ideal Learning Situation
Instant Messenger (IM)	• Impromptu one-to-one assistance • Just-in-time support and guidance • Homework help • Scheduled office hours • Small team communication • Collaboration on group projects • Paired scenario-based activities • Reference or technical support
Chat Room	• Scheduled office hours • Q&A with guest experts or instructor • Group scenario-based dialogues • Peer discussion on course material • Facilitated discussion by instructor • Organizing meetings for team projects
MUVE	• Game-based learning activities • Role-playing activities • Group problem-solving simulations • Exploration of virtual worlds • Team-building activities
Virtual Reference Desk	• One-to-one reference support • One-to-one mentoring or coaching • One-to-one tutoring • One-to-one advising • Q&A for prospective students • Technical support • Scheduled drop-in hours
Virtual Office/ Meeting Room	• Group meetings • Office hours • Team or group discussions and work • Impromptu or planned gatherings • Recurring office hours • Review sessions • Show and tell sessions

Venue	Ideal Learning Situation
Virtual Classroom	• Scheduled class lessons • Formal instructor-led presentations • Interactive seminars • Student-led presentations • Critique sessions • Facilitated labs or problem solving • Organized breakout sessions
Interactive Webcasting	• Large group lessons or lectures • Simulcasts from face-to-face events • Public events with high-profile experts • Panel-led sessions with Q&A • Virtual tours or information sessions • Keynote addresses • Program launches or conferences
Broadcasting	• Large event simulcasts • Lecture broadcasts • High-profile speakers • Commencement addresses • Live news events
In-Class Online Aids	• Hands-on Web exploration • Remote student or expert participation • Virtual labs • Interactive diagrams or animations • Group collaboration • Question submission • Quizzing and polling • Synchronized note taking

as slide showing or Web touring functions, but are usually distinguished by the fact that text messages are the primary channel of real-time communication.

Chat rooms are also one of the oldest forums for real-time, Internet-based communication. The first chat venue used widely among those in the computer world may have been something called the "talk" facility in the Unix operating system, which allows messages to be sent to another person's computer screen, with each letter showing up as it is typed by the remote sender. This tool has not been used widely in online instruction, outside, perhaps, computer science courses. In the 1980s, people accessing the Internet through commerical dial-up services such as Compuserve or connecting directly into a bulletin board service (BBS) used chat room facilities to communicate via text with others logged in at the same time. In 1988, a text-based chat system called Internet Relay Chat, or IRC, appeared and has served as the underlying protocol on which many online chat systems are now based or modeled.

Many systems for putting courses online today include a basic chat room utility, which is used by some instructors to conduct office hours, provide online guidance, or otherwise encourage real-time communication among their students.

INSTANT MESSENGER

An instant messenger is primarily a one-to-one venue for the real-time exchange of impromptu messages. Although traditionally a text-based medium, voice-based instant messaging has grown rapidly in popularity, especially since it is a free and convenient way to circumvent long distance telephone charges. Most instant messengers do permit spur-of-the-moment group meetings with more than two participants, but are not the tool of choice for more than a very small handful of people due largely to instability at larger numbers.

One of the distinguishing elements of instant messengers is a *presence indicator,* whereby one can instantly gauge the availability of another person for an online conversation at any moment. People who use instant messengers tend to be connected to them throughout the day from their computers or their Web-enabled mobile telephones (which also support instant messaging functions). They will use the tool to indicate whether they are available, away, busy, or on the phone, which gives others a sense of their willingness or readiness to interact.

A dynamic and ongoing portrayal of one's online presence or status, combined with the ubiquity and simplicity of these tools, has made instant messengers an invaluable resource for getting just-in-time information and support. Instant messaging is used increasingly in the workplace (Shiu and Lenhart, 2004), and is becoming an indispensable "lifeline" by which people tap into their social and professional networks to share and provide information at the moment of need.

Use of instant messaging to support courses or other formal instruction taps into a freely available, collaborative communication channel that promises to make people as important as search engines when it comes to finding the information one needs to proceed with a learning task at hand.

In educational contexts, the use of instant messengers among peers encourages active learning, team-based collaboration, and prompt feedback (Cunliffe, 2005). The technology is being used for team projects, study groups, peer-to-peer homework assistance, tutoring and mentoring, office hours, technical support, and ad hoc in-line discussions about course content. A substantial number of students are even using instant messenger to communicate with peers in the same physical classroom (Shiu and Lenhart, 2004), or as a private back-channel while they are using other forms of communication, such as chat rooms, virtual classrooms, or telephone conference calls.

MULTI-USER VIRTUAL ENVIRONMENTS

Multi-user virtual environments (MUVEs) support independent and group exploration of shared virtual spaces, which are usually characterized by three-dimensional renderings of imagined or real-world places. Communication among "occupants" of these worlds can be via text, animated gestures or movement, and increasingly audio, as is the case with many Web-connected video games. The people using MUVEs are often represented on screen by avatars or self-selected characters. As a learner navigates from room to room or landscape to landscape, he or she can interact with other people and examine objects found in the scene. Pre-programmed avatars or *bots* might complement those characters operated by live humans and employ artificial intelligence engines to respond to questions and provide guidance.

In educational situations, MUVEs can combine the engaging graphics of video games, the authenticity of field work and exposure to primary sources, and the social aspects of team-based projects to produce immersive problem-solving activities. Crafting successful learning experiences to take place in MUVEs requires the ability to define a problem suitable for exploration in such an environment and to think in three dimensions. Learning objectives that require group problem-solving skills, and the ability to collect, analyze, and synthesize clues, might be good candidates for these virtual worlds. One key to achieving good learner results in MUVEs is to provide enough variety in terms of scenes and objects to maintain interest long enough for a problem to be solved. If a virtual world lacks sufficient and appropriate complexity, learners may grow frustrated with the environment as a suitable playground and venue.

Proponents of MUVEs in education suggest that they allow learners to interact with each other online in a safe environment that they have helped construct (Cooper, 2003). They may also be a way to help learners transfer what they learn in an academic context to real-world settings (Harvard GSE, 2003). Work by Dede and Ketelhut (2003) suggests that immersive and interactive simulations, like the virtual museum exhibits and "participatory" historical scenarios they conducted with learners in MUVEs, may help improve motivation and achievement of low-performing students. At the very least, these environments offer another available venue in which we can attempt to craft engaging and meaningful live experiences for learners increasingly accustomed to interacting in digital worlds for work and play.

VIRTUAL REFERENCE, TUTORING, AND HELP DESKS

Online reference desks, tutoring, or advising venues specialize in enabling one-to-one communication between an expert and a student, patron, or Web site visitor seeking support or guidance. Although instant messengers and chat rooms can be used for these purposes, virtual reference desks and other one-on-one virtual advising platforms often include specialized tools to allow the expert or support staff person to better handle frequently asked questions and guide the information seeker to relevant resources. Online learner support provided through these kinds of venues often includes things such as

- A queuing system to route visitors to an appropriate and available expert
- The ability to easily save and send session transcripts to the information seeker
- Pre-set answers and scripts that can be used for common requests
- Web page touring and application sharing to bring needed resources right to the learner

Tools focused on tutoring and coaching might also include a virtual whiteboard for illustrating vocal or text-based explanations, and preloaded slides or diagrams based on frequent or timely topics.

It is well documented that individualized attention, support, and advising improves student retention and contributes to the success of distance learners in achieving their educational objectives (Ludwig-Hardman and Dunlap, 2003). Colleges and universities serving online learners offer a growing array of communication channels—many of them online—for connecting with learners, beginning with admission guidance and financial aid support and continuing throughout an entire educational program with course advising, tutoring, library reference assistance, and career counseling. Real-time online tools enable all of these kinds of personalized support services to be offered seamlessly in a just-in-time manner within the overall learning environment.

Virtual reference desks may be staffed by library staff at particular hours noted on an institution's portal or library pages. Real-time online tutoring and academic advising services may also be of a "drop-in" nature or can be by appointment. Personalized support venues often have a dynamic status indicator component that can be placed on a course or department Web site to automatically indicate when an expert or counselor is "live online now" to assist.

When combined with a growing number of campus initiatives to improve online learner retention and provide personalized online student support services, the dramatic uptake in the use of synchronous tools for just-in-time assistance suggests that this expert-to-learner style of real-time venue is becoming a central fixture of the online academic environment.

VIRTUAL OFFICES AND VIRTUAL MEETING ROOMS

Virtual offices provide an online real-time venue for small group gatherings, such as office hours, meetings, tutorials, informal discussions, or team collaboration sessions. A virtual office tends to "belong" to an individual, have a Web address that remains consistent over time, and act as his or her virtual headquarters on the Web. These virtual spaces, which are good for both planned and ad hoc meetings, usually include shared virtual whiteboards and text messaging tools, as well as VoIP audio and video options. They are also commonly used in conjunction with telephone conference calls. Although some virtual offices have recording functionality, it is less common for one to want to capture the informal goings-on of a meeting or drop-in session than a more formal class activity that might occur in a different venue.

Within an online course, student groups or teams might each be allocated a discrete virtual meeting or conference room to gather online and work on collaborative projects. For an instructor, a virtual office can establish a consistent place where he or she can be found at particular times, fostering a sense among learners—especially those in completely distance-based courses—that their instructor is accessible and available to provide personalized guidance and support throughout the course. Teaching assistants might also use a virtual office to lead office hours, smaller group discussions, or exam review sessions. We know that the availability of student services like these supports and develops learning, has a positive impact on student emotion and confidence, and helps students deal with institutional rules and requirements in ways that encourage retention (Tait, 2003). Tools such as virtual offices and virtual meeting rooms are well suited for achieving these goals and enhancing student service offerings.

In instructional settings, virtual offices are also indispensable tools for interacting with members of the academic community outside the context of an online course. Drop-in hours, planned tutorials, or meetings for financial aid advising, career counseling, or admission questions and answers can all be held live online to meet the needs of learners and prospective students who are increasingly looking to the institution's Web presence for answers and assistance.

VIRTUAL CLASSROOMS

As the name suggests, a virtual classroom is the venue most likely to include digital counterparts for all of the key resources available in a traditional physical classroom. A virtual classroom is often characterized by

- Real-time voice and visual contact between all participants
- A shared whiteboard
- An integrated area for the projection of slides or other visuals
- The capacity for text-based interaction, including side conversations or note-passing
- A means for learners to indicate they have questions or are confused
- Tools for assessing current moods, opinions, and comprehension and for soliciting questions or feedback
- The ability to gauge virtual body language, or a sense of how engaged learners are in the activity at hand

Internet-based videoconferencing systems that comprise a similar set of tools are often considered virtual classrooms as well.

A virtual classroom is well-equipped to take on a central role in the delivery of a course. Whereas less full-featured real-time venues may be better suited to serve in ancillary capacities in support of overall instruction, a virtual classroom is a practical venue for live classes, activities, or gatherings that are actually the main anchor points of an entire course. This is not to say that virtual classrooms are always used in this manner, but their versatility and capacity for supporting a broad range of human interaction among learners—with voice, video, graphics, and text—positions them well to serve in a primary role.

When virtual classrooms play a recurring and formal role in an overall course structure, they help foster an ongoing relationship with students and a group dynamic that builds from one live online session to the next. Instructors in face-to-face classes that meet regularly will look out at a classroom—where students often take the same seats—and begin to notice which students are first to raise their hands and which ones require more prompting before they will speak. In virtual classrooms, patterns and personalities also emerge in real time. Used effectively in combination with other online course tools, a virtual classroom can become the same kind of headquarters for learning as a well-utilized physical classroom.

There is often an expectation in a physical classroom that all participants will be called upon to actively participate in the class activity in a meaningful way at one time or another. In a virtual classroom that is being used in an interactive manner, there is similarly little opportunity for student anonymity or for hiding in the back of the classroom. The larger the number of participants assembled, the more difficult it is for each learner to receive individualized, real-time feedback from the instructor. Virtual classroom sessions generally best support, technologically and pedagogically, small to medium-sized groups.

INTERACTIVE WEBCASTING

Live interactive Webcast venues are designed to reach larger groups of people while maintaining the ability for participants to offer some degree of individual or collective real-time feedback and influence the direction of the session. As the word's stem suggests, Web*casts* are frequently weighted more toward the casting out of information from a central point than the cultivation of a common group discussion in which the presenter and participants are equally involved. This is not to say that interactive Webcasts cannot generate intense real-time discussion; they certainly can. The degree to which that discussion is elevated to be the primary focus of the live experience, however, depends on skillful facilitation and remains limited by the large number of people and perspectives present.

Interactive Webcasts are often characterized by

- Broadcasting of live audio or video from one or a small handful of presenters
- Synchronized display of visuals such as slides, Web sites, or applications
- Channels for limited or controlled participant feedback, such as text messaging to the moderator
- Group polls and surveys

Although audio- or video-based comments from participants are sometimes possible in these venues, it is less practical to engage in full two-way voice discussions during interactive Webcasts than during smaller scale virtual classroom sessions. Interactive Webcasts often have more than one "addressable" viewing area, meaning that someone "producing" an activity in this kind of venue might be able to show content slides in one window, speaker biographies in another, and the logo of a sponsoring institution in a different part of the interface.

An interactive Webcast venue is ideal for situations with large numbers of participants in which there is a need to balance an acceptable level of order with an appropriate level of interactivity. Examples might include

- Live panel discussions
- Debates among pairs of remotely located experts
- Appearances by high-profile or celebrity guest speakers
- Informational sessions
- Town hall–style meetings
- The live transmission or simulcast of large-scale, face-to-face presentations to remotely located online participants, with the ability for both audiences to pose questions or provide some level of real-time feedback

Interactive Webcasts can involve the coordination of many people and detailed logistics. For this reason, an activity that takes place in these real-time venues can be called an "event," which connotes something requiring a fair amount of planning or production work to orchestrate, both before and during the Webcast.

Virtual classroom and interactive Webcast venues tend to have a similar set of synchronous tools available, but the latter usually exposes them in a more moderated way. For example, in an interactive Webcast environment, a question submitted as a text message from a participant may not automatically be displayed publicly for all to see. It might first need to be approved or recognized by the presenter or a panelist, who often has a special interface to review comments or a queue of questions before sharing them with the whole group (if the presenter should decide to acknowledge them at all).

It is difficult to specify the class size at which a virtual classroom session becomes an interactive Webcast event. That really depends on the nature of the material being explored, the lesson activity itself, and an instructor's own ability to maintain a sense of intimacy and a feeling among learners that their presence matters—even as the size of the audience grows. It is usually easier for a student to avoid being called upon in an interactive Webcast environment than in a virtual classroom, as would be the case with most offline lecture halls. This is not to say that student accountability is lacking in a large interactive Webcast venue. There are increasingly robust tools for measuring participation in all kinds of synchronous venues, including interactive Webcast platforms.

It should be noted that there are virtual classroom platforms that can ably support interactive Webcasts, and visa versa. Although naming conventions are far less important than how we actually use these virtual venues for instruction, it is important to make conscious decisions about the kind of learning experience we are trying to foster and choose environments that will best be suited for the undertaking.

WEBCASTING OR BROADCASTING

When opportunities to interact in real time are absent, Webcasting is essentially just the broadcasting of a one-way, live audio or video feed over the Internet to a group of "listeners" or "viewers" (which might be more suitable names than "participants"). Although digital convergence brings some additional tools to bear to enhance the transmission—such as synchronizing slides to the audio or "pushing" out Web pages for viewers to navigate in real-time—pure Webcasting serves a function very similar to traditional television or radio broadcasting. One major and notable difference is that Webcasting can be transmitted from virtually any computer, and received by anyone with any Internet connection, regardless of geography. Traditional broadcasting requires expensive equipment and transmission methods and can often only be picked up in certain parts of the world, whereas Webcasting can originate in a garage in Duluth and be viewed nearly instantaneously in a classroom in Delhi.

When used by an instructor in the context of an online class, live Webcasting essentially enables the delivery of Web-based lectures or broadcasts. The success of a live Webcast relies heavily on the

- Compelling or engaging nature of the content
- Time-sensitivity of the message
- Special nature of the speaker
- Authenticity of its originating location
- And above all else, the defensibility of the rationale for doing it live

Without real-time opportunities to interact with the presenter, instructor, or peers, one must always consider whether a recording or other asynchronous delivery would be as or more effective than a live Webcast. This kind of consideration respects learners and the individual time commitments their lives dictate. There are times for self-directed exploration and guided live experiences, but we serve our students better when we don't confuse the two.

Live Webcasting can be used with success in several situations. Instructors in face-to-face or online teaching scenarios tap into a live Webcast to allow learners to witness an event of interest unfolding elsewhere. This can lend to the authenticity of the learning experience and connect course-based themes with real-world stories. For example, watching live segments of political debates, space missions, trial testimony, or surgical operations together as a class can provide the impetus for immediate discussion and the localized exploration of a global theme to the class topic at hand. Complementing a live Webcast with a basic text chat room or virtual meeting room application can allow distance learners to digest and respond in real time as a group to the primary source unfolding before them. Instructors can wrap their own live lessons around other live content on the Web to great effect.

Live Webcasting can also be used to provide dispatches from interesting places, live on-location greetings from or interviews with intriguing people of interest, or a brief element of excitement to a course. Webcasts can also extend a physical classroom-based experience to online learners unable to be present on site. Although there is a growing breed of specialized Web-based tools designed specifically for connecting face-to-face classrooms with distance-based learners in an interactive manner, basic Webcasting can be a simple way to give non-campus-based learners the option not to miss a live class.

IN-CLASS ONLINE AIDS

Any of the synchronous venues described so far for completely online communication may also be deployed intelligently within a physical classroom to enhance the face-to-face learning experience. Although instant messengers are now a common back-channel for students to converse or pass electronic notes to each other in class, live online tools can also be leveraged in a more formal way by instructors to foster group collaboration and engaging experiences within the physical classroom. The idea of conducting computer-mediated, in-person activities is not brand new. A concept called *group support systems* (GSS) became an area of considerable research in the 1980s. GSS employ a range of technology-based tools to facilitate group problem solving and decision making (DeSanctis and Gallupe, 1987).

Although there have been some institutions and organizations that have taken to this approach over the years, a few recent trends in today's computing environment are making computer-facilitated, face-to-face activities more feasible to employ today than in any time in the past. First, the proliferation of mobile computing devices such as personal digital assistants (PDAs), cell phones, and laptops means that virtually any setting can be home to a technology-mediated lesson; gone is the era when all participants would have no choice but to congregate in a special computer lab. The easing of restrictions on the venue opens many doors for new kinds of learning activities. Second, the rampant growth of wireless connectivity to networks and the Internet makes portable devices useful in a group setting, where each person can connect to and interact with common resources. Furthermore, the increase in the number of free and commercially available synchronous tools has meant that the integration of connected devices into group learning situations can be done meaningfully by any creative instructor who sets his or her mind to it. If the students are already instant-messaging with each other during class, the potential is there to harness these proclivities and focus them on the learning objective at hand.

Reinig, Briggs, and Nunamaker, citing a range of work on the subject, summarized that "research has shown that group support systems . . . can improve the classroom experience. In a variety of studies, GSS have been shown to increase observed learning, self-reported learning, on-task participation, and satisfaction with the classroom experience" (1997–1998). In our Internet-based world today, in-class aids can be effective learning tools, but success depends on a facilitator with a clear sense of how and why "gizmos" are being used.

The use of synchronous tools in physical settings can range from an auxiliary role to a very central one. In some situations, a chat room or text messaging application can be used as an additional "channel" for submitting questions to instructor. As a student thinks of a question, he or she submits it online without interrupting the speaker. At appropriate intervals, the facilitator glances at a screen and sees a queue of questions and looks for common themes. Some points are addressed in class, some seed a class discussion, and others are saved for after class when the instructor responds in an asynchronous class discussion forum. Taken a step further, an instructor might present a question or scenario and ask all students to respond at the same time via a chat tool. In the absence of a computing device, the class leader would not necessarily have time to receive vocal responses from all students, but in this kind of scenario an instructor can collect feedback from all learners, ask some to elaborate vocally, and even choose to save responses for assessment purposes or to gauge participation later. The possibilities for engaging all learners at the same time and keeping everyone alert and thinking critically offers some unique possibilities for changing the nature of classroom learning.

A new crop of Web-based synchronous tools are being brought to the market and are specialized for mediating group interaction in physical settings. Like some of the earlier GSS applications, the new venues include special templates for group brainstorming, topic outlining, mind mapping, and decision making. Some record the class for later playback by students and simulcast the in-class activities online so that remote participants may also take part.

Facilitating Learning in Real Time

As Bert Kimura noted: "No matter what technology we employ, it is still the human experience that is most important. Students learn from teachers, their peers and knowledge experts. No one learns from a computer" (2002, retrieved May 2005). And Pak Yoong (1995), citing McGoff and Ambrose (1991), confirms for us what we probably all intuitively know: "Although the technology has matured . . . our experience continues to confirm that the quality of [a] group session is predominantly dependent on the facilitator" (p. 1). Although that notion was put forth before Web-based synchronous tools burgeoned, it was true then and it remains true today. Computers don't teach people; people teach people.

In early 1999, the department head of a large institution that had just bought a live virtual classroom platform invited an education consultant to her campus to meet with a group of instructors. Before the meeting started, all of the instructors appeared terribly nervous. A few were biting their nails, a handful had sweat on their brow, and one was grinding his teeth. None looked happy to be there. They had

heard through the grapevine that a new computer system had been installed that facilitated live classes. The instructors assumed the worst—automation—and that they
were all gathered so that they could be fired by the person who installed the system that was to replace them.

The truth was a welcome surprise to all of them. This "computer system" did
not make them irrelevant. It made them more important than ever. They were
going to have the opportunity to share their passion for their respective subject
areas with learners in remote locations who otherwise would not have had convenient access to them and their expertise. Understanding the situation, they all
now saw it as an exciting opportunity, but not one without challenges. The
instructors understood they would need to evaluate their personal approach to
teaching to see how it could be translated to the live online realm, or perhaps even
be improved because of it.

This chapter offers practical strategies for facilitating live online learning activities. It contains overarching principles to help ensure that live sessions are led
interactively and effectively, and offers guidance to achieving a comfort level in
teaching in the synchronous realm.

BE A GOOD HOST

One of the most basic tenets of good live online facilitation is to be a good host.
An effective live online leader is similar in many regards to the host of a successful dinner party (Table 5.1). One prepares for the guests' arrival, welcomes them
warmly, frequently assesses the mood in the room and anticipates guests' needs,
makes everyone feel included, facilitates connections and conversation, offers guests
something to take home with them, knows when to say good night, and leaves
everyone wanting more so they will want to return when next invited.

In a synchronous environment, one must never lose sight of the fact that learners are present. When a bit nervous about being in a new online environment and
looking at a computer screen—and not out at a room full of faces—it is conceiv-
able that one can forget, even momentarily, that there are actual people congregated to participate virtually. By building interaction into the agenda, and
cultivating a sense of community right from the outset of the session, one is much
less likely to fall into an "autopilot" mode in which opportunities to take advantage of the presence of real people in real time are neglected.

Table 5.1. Being a "Good Host" in Synchronous Sessions.

Dinner Party Axiom	Live Online Learning Guidance
Prepare for your guests' arrival	Have the resources that you plan to use ready in advance so that you can begin on time. When learners arrive, you want to be able to focus on them and on the content and collaboration at hand.
Welcome guests warmly	As people login, welcome each person by name if possible. In addition to being a warm way to begin, it sets a tone and reminds learners that you know they are present and that their participation will be expected.
Frequently assess the mood in the room; don't wait until the end to ask guests if they need anything	Periodically gauge comprehension and mood by asking quick poll questions, soliciting emoticon use, or cold-calling on learners for feedback. Waiting until the last few minutes leaves little opportunity for adjustment.
Have more food (for thought) than you need	Prepare more activities than you think are needed for the time allotted. It is better to have a few planned activities left over for next time than to be short of things to do together as a group, thereby causing learners to question why they needed to carve the same hour out of their day.
Make everyone feel included	Try to recognize and solicit contributions from as many participants as possible, and refer to comments made by the name of the person who shared them. This is even more important online than offline, where multiple voices can be heard at once and some can be lost in the mix.
Facilitate connections and conversation, but don't dominate every discussion	Use your role as facilitator to foster an environment where learners are exchanging ideas with others, and seeing their peers as resources for ongoing learning. If a lecture is needed, consider recording it and posting it to a course site for anytime viewing rather than doing it live.
Offer guests something to take home with them	In combination with a transcript or recording of a live online session, post handouts, slides, or the results of group activities as on-demand resources within a course site. These convenient take-aways help reinforce new knowledge constructed or shared during the experience.
Know when to say good night; leave everyone wanting more	End on a high point. Don't cram too much into a live session or preside over unnecessarily long goodbyes. If a session peters out, participant attention will diminish quickly and goodwill can suffer. Conclude at a high-energy level to propel learners to do their follow-up work and keep them excited about the next live session.

INFLATE A BUBBLE OF CONCENTRATION

Few things can help a facilitator stay better attuned to learner progress and feedback in real-time sessions online than a deliberate effort on the part of the instructor to maintain focus on the experience. The online environment offers many ongoing and constantly changing indicators about how successfully a session is meeting its objectives. Minimizing external distractions, both online and off, can help the instructor pick up on those cues, adapt accordingly, and realize the full potential of the time spent together with learners.

By consciously inflating an imaginary bubble around yourself at the outset of a live online session and extending it around your computer screen, keyboard, and mouse, you can help block out environmental activity that might cause you to lose focus on the people at hand. Closing unneeded applications, turning off telephone ringers, and closing an office door can also help in this regard. If using a venue that includes audio, a pair of headphones can be worn to minimize external noises and keep the focus on online participants.

One approach to inflating a bubble of concentration is to ask all participants at the outset of a session to identify potential distractions around them and enter them into the text messaging area or onto the whiteboard. In addition to some of the expected responses—such as "telephone ringing," "e-mail," "people coming by my desk"—one will almost always get a few more unusual or personal responses. These might include: "the sun is shining through my window," "boss is yelling at a colleague," "it's my birthday," "open bottle of wine on my desk." Invite the participants to consciously think about how they are going to minimize or avoid each distraction for the duration of the session. By getting these possible disruptions all out on the table at the outset, one accomplishes a few things:

- Neutralizes the distractions at each site by actively assisting each person to recognize them
- Demonstrates that the instructor recognizes that each person is an individual, each in unique surroundings
- Builds a sense of community among all those present

This activity only takes a minute or two, yet one would probably not repeat this activity each time with the same group. One might, however, reference it briefly to reinforce the need to inflate a bubble of concentration for the duration of the live session.

Figure 5.1 illustrates an example of this simple "Distractions Around Us" activity on the virtual whiteboard.

BE A RINGMASTER

Most synchronous venues feature more than one channel of communication that can be used concurrently. Through multiple conduits participants can communicate, interact, share visuals, and exchange ideas and files all at the same time. Someone might be speaking with live audio, while others are sending public and private text messages, showing Web pages, and sharing applications, video, or other multimedia content. If all of these channels are engaged at the same time, it can feel like a three ring circus. But even a circus with three rings has a ringmaster. The

Figure 5.1. Sample "Distractions Around Us" Whiteboard Screen.

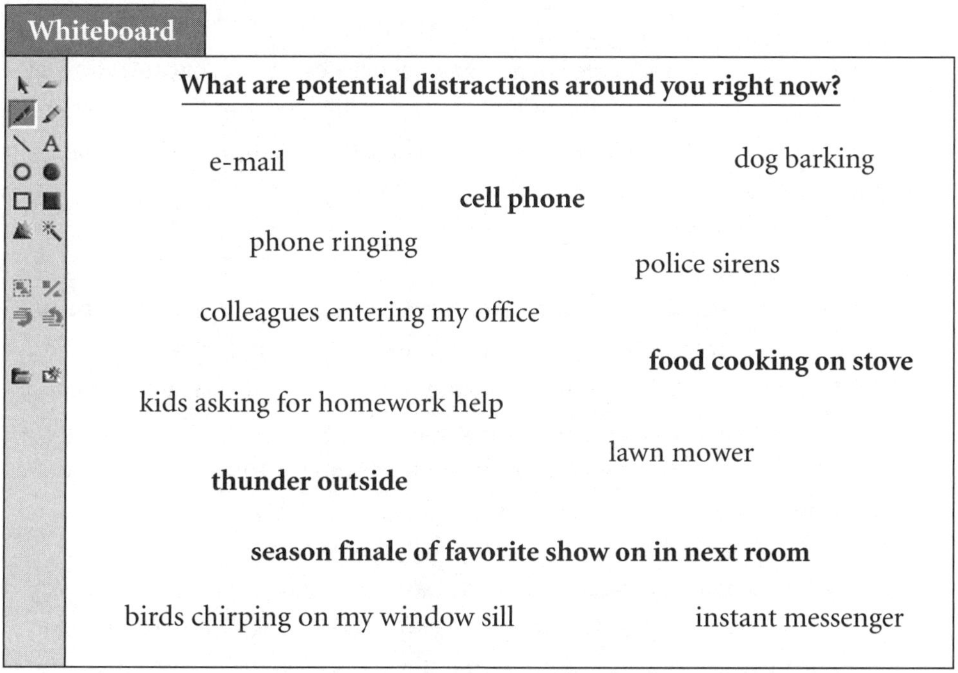

What are potential distractions around you right now?

e-mail   dog barking

cell phone

phone ringing

police sirens

colleagues entering my office

food cooking on stove

kids asking for homework help

lawn mower

thunder outside

season finale of favorite show on in next room

birds chirping on my window sill   instant messenger

ringmaster is the person who focuses the attention of a circus audience to a specific ring or area of the tent at a particular time.

However, we might not want to draw parallels comparing our learning activities to a circus; the metaphor—when it comes to academic environments—has a somewhat negative connotation. Yet circuses are stimulating and interactive experiences that engage the senses; so to that extent, they may not be a bad model for an online learning activity. In the hands of a ringmaster, a circus is quite organized, even if there is much going on. There can be much going on in a synchronous learning venue as well, so we can learn a few things from a ringmaster about good facilitation in our online environments.

Specify and Maintain Focus

A live online facilitator has a range of ways to focus his or her learners on the activity or content at hand. The simplest thing to do is to state outright what method learners should be using to participate at a particular time. The method can change throughout a given learning activity (one part of a lesson might include use of a whiteboard to share ideas, and a subsequent experience might move to the text chat area for discussion), but a facilitator should be explicit about where the focus should be at any given point. This is where the existence of a bubble of concentration helps most; if learners are already in a deliberate state of concentration, signals from the facilitator to focus on one aspect of the environment will be more readily parlayed into practice. Exhibit 5.1 provides some sample phrases that help keep the spotlight where it needs to be at any given time.

Setting Ground Rules

One can also specify a set of ground rules regarding which "rings" should be used for which kinds of interaction throughout a session. As an illustration, consider an activity from a course on public speaking in which a pair of students is asked to defend opposing positions on a controversial topic during a synchronous, audio-based debate. The instructor sets forth these guidelines for the students observing the debate online:

> During the debate, please use the *text messaging* box in real-time to post constructive feedback regarding the *form* or *style* of each debater's argument. Begin your text comment with *P* if it is directed at the pro speaker

Exhibit 5.1. Example Phrases of the Live Online Ringmaster.

Here are a few examples of phrases that can help keep the spotlight where it needs to be in a synchronous environment at any given time. Think about what you can say during your live online sessions that directs learner attention to where it should be at a given moment. This can help participants who might otherwise be overwhelmed by all of the places possible to focus.

- "Let's all turn our attention to the text chat area."
- "I am going to turn off audio and video for a few minutes. Please respond to the question that you see on the screen now by typing on the whiteboard."
- "Please do not send private messages to each other right now. We should all be listening to John and Lizzie as they share their story."
- "Please watch Suzanne show her project using application sharing. Hold off for the next few minutes on making any comments that do not pertain directly to what Suzanne is showing us."
- "I am now opening a new Web page window on each person's screen. Please click the 'yes' button when you have finished reviewing the top paragraph to let me know you are ready to discuss."
- "Let's all pause and read through the great comments that have been entered in the chat room. Please hold off on adding anything new for the next two minutes as we all reflect on the points submitted so far."
- "Reynaldo, please take the microphone and read the poem aloud that appears on the screen. Everyone else, please follow along and say the words along with him. Even though we will only hear Reynaldo, I want everyone reading and saying these words aloud."
- "On your screen you will see a map of Sudan and a window with a video clip. As I play the short video for you, please circle the area of the map to which the video is referring. We'll debrief in a moment. Unless there are questions now, let's keep the chat area quiet until we are done with the map activity."

and C if it is meant for the con speaker. On the *whiteboard* you'll see I have a two-column table labeled *pro* and *con* [Figure 5.2]. Use the whiteboard during the debate to place a mark in the appropriate column each time you think a speaker earns a point on the *substance* of their argument. Please don't use these tools for any other purpose during the seven-minute debate. We'll all do an *audio* debriefing using the microphone after this pair of speakers wraps up their debate.

Figure 5.2. Pro-Con Exercise.

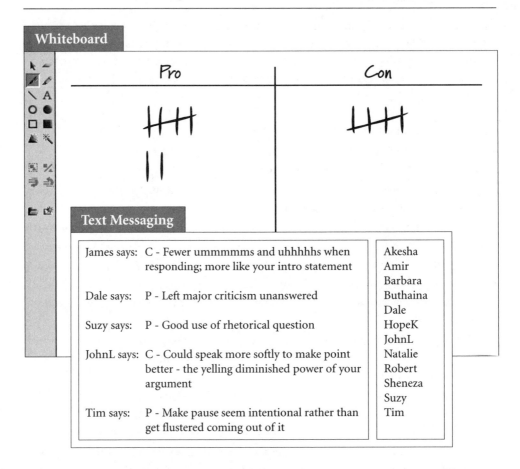

Note in the above scenario that different tools are being earmarked for different instructional purposes, and the facilitator is explicitly asking participants to refrain from communicating in ways other than those prescribed.

Using Technical Means to Focus Attention

Directing participant focus can be accomplished by technical means, as well as by verbal instructions. Some platforms allow a live online facilitator to disable certain tools as needed. For example, one might temporarily turn off the ability to send public text messages, mute all audio controls, lock the visuals onto one slide, and then ask all participants to use a virtual pen tool to mark up a geometry diagram or piece of artwork displayed in the whiteboard. At this point, there is but one place to focus.

Other computer-mediated approaches to maintaining focus include using a whiteboard tool and its virtual laser pointer to figuratively gesture toward the center of activity. Some venues allow facilitators to display their mouse moving over any part of the interface to direct participants' attention. One could even do this more literally when on camera using live video, by actually pointing or looking toward the area of the screen where you would like learners to turn their gaze. This approach often elicits smiles but does the job nicely.

Manage Sideshows

A sideshow at a circus is usually outside the main tent and features something that complements, but is not, the main exhibition. Sideshow activity during a live online event or lesson—such as ongoing text chat while an instructor is speaking—should be explicitly managed, channeled appropriately, or curtailed by the facilitator, depending on the situation.

Nonrelevant conversations should usually be taken offline or to a private channel, and facilitators should feel comfortable saying as much. There is more of a gray area, however, when it comes to activity that pertains to the current session but is not currently in the spotlight, such as tangential discussions spawned by class activities. As an instructor, one needs to balance one's own comfort with sidebar activity with learner engagement. Sidebar activity may be desirable by some participants but distracting to others. In some situations, it can be suitable to ask participants to hold off on providing any input other than what is specifically solicited by the facilitator. Other times, participants can be encouraged to be more spontaneous and share questions or comments as they occur to them. The latter can provide a healthy view into the minds of learners in real time in a way that is not possible in asynchronous means. Spontaneity and a real-time "let's see where this takes us" approach are hallmarks of synchronous online venues and can lead to meaningful learning experiences online just as they can offline. The bottom line is that more than one approach can be used—even during the same synchronous sessions—and an instructor should simply be clear about the current rules of engagement as they change.

In most online academic settings with young adult or adult learners, participants will respond well and adhere to verbal guidelines set out clearly by the facilitator.

When they do not, computer-mediated tools can be used to disable certain channels of communication for the group or the offending individuals. For example, most people will respect the wishes of an instructor who says, "Let's hold off on the text messaging for the next few moments and focus on Alessandro as he demonstrates his project for us."

Learner Styles and Preferences

While acting as a ringmaster and making decisions to turn on and off or focus attention on certain channels of communication over others, it is important to bear in mind one of the great advantages of many synchronous environments. Multiple modes for learner input means learners have the ability to choose from a variety of options that are suitable to their individual learning style or preference. Given a choice, students will select a means of contributing that feels most comfortable to them. For example, some will prefer speaking with a microphone to typing; others will opt for a text-based response over a spoken one. When appropriate, a facilitator can usually maximize overall participation by presenting participants with alternative forms of providing input. Of course, too many choices can also be paralyzing to some learners, and so a specific default option is usually a good idea as well.

If It Drops, Pick It Up

When distractions crop up during a live session (for example, a student types an inappropriate comment igniting a disruptive dialogue, or there is some noise heard in the background because an instructor's neighbor is mowing her lawn), one tendency is to ignore them and hope they go away. Another tack is to confront them head-on, neutralize them, and move on with everyone's focus recentered.

The single most important piece of guidance in dealing with these situations comes from Emil Maurer, an English teacher who also directed school plays. He shared with his student actors a simple piece of advice not foreign to those trained in the theater: "If something falls, pick it up." In other words, if you are performing and a prop—a hat, for example—accidentally falls on the stage, simply pick it up. Untrained actors will often get nervous, pretend it did not happen, and leave the hat on the floor. Meanwhile, each audience member is sidetracked by the hat and no one is watching the show. In real life, when something falls, we retrieve it uneventfully and we move on, and in a computer-mediated, live online environment, we

need to do the same. Here is one example of how an instructor manages a potential distraction and keeps learners focused:

> An instructor is leading a math seminar with his students in an audio-
> enabled virtual classroom and a baby is heard crying in the background
> while the instructor is speaking. He makes no mention of the crying and
> all of the learners begin to think to themselves, "I wonder how old the
> baby is? I think it's a girl. No, it sounds like a boy. Maybe it is hungry. Is
> he ignoring his baby? What kind of father is he?!" No one is paying any
> attention to the instructor's lesson.

Rather than pretend the baby is not there, and make no mention of it, the instructor should be proactive and neutralize the situation with a brief, but candid,
description of what is happening. For example: "My apologies, students. That's my
fourteen-month-old, Tiffany. My partner is putting her to bed. It's past her bed
time. She'll be asleep in no time. The joys of distance learning and teaching from
home! Now, who can tell me the length of the hypotenuse in this example?" The
result is that the learners are less distracted, and the instructor is perceived as being
more human. The more human the learning environment, the more likely people
are to learn (Knowles, 1990).

USE VIRTUAL BODY LANGUAGE

Nonverbal messages and actions are an important facet of face-to-face interpersonal communication, a notion supported by a large body of literature on the subject. It just makes sense that what we *do* can matter as much as what we *say* when
we are communicating with others. Anyone who has been the subject of a silent
glance from a professor upon trying to quietly enter a classroom fifteen minutes
late knows that. And when third-grader Jonathan Finkelstein heard his teacher tell
the class that she was going to start the lesson over "because Jonathan does not
quite get this yet," he learned how the unwitting squinting of his left eye—if
detected by an astute observer and a great educator—could change the course of
an afternoon for an entire class, and at least one person's understanding of math.

One of the characteristics of nonverbal communication that can make it a useful tool to educators is something called *immediacy*. Albert Mehrabian (1969)
defined immediacy behaviors in communication as those behaviors that "enhance

closeness to and nonverbal interaction with another." In other words, things like facial expressions, eye contact, tone of voice, movement, proximity, posture, stance, and gestures can all affect the degree to which people feel close to others. In citing a wide body of research tying immediacy to instruction, Baringer and McCroskey (2000) remind us that "when teachers are immediate with their students, this behavior results in numerous positive outcomes" (p. 179).

Exchanging Nonverbal Cues in Synchronous Settings

Face-to-face settings clearly offer opportunities to enhance verbal language communication with simultaneous channels for exchanging nonverbal signals, but synchronous online learning environments also offer us simultaneous channels—albeit somewhat different—for sharing information that enhances the verbal experience. Group whiteboards, text chat back channels, presence indicators, and emoticons are just some of the tools available for expression that are just as absent from most physical settings as, for example, the ability to stand on a desk for emphasis is missing from most virtual ones. Both settings are no doubt rich in communication options.

One of our goals when leading synchronous instructional activities should be to look for ways to achieve levels of immediacy with our students, whether through the nonverbal *or* verbal means at our disposal, that achieve our learning objectives and create an environment conducive to learning. What we are seeking are forms of virtual body language that help us connect and better respond to learners, or what Jennifer Hofmann (2004b) refers to as the "body language in the bandwidth."

It is worth keeping in mind as we explore virtual "body language" that when one is using a synchronous tool to communicate online, it is presumably because

1. Live communication and interaction is best suited to achieve the learning objective.
2. Distance or logistics are an obstacle to conducting the activity face-to-face.

In other words, we are assuming that if a group could feasibly meet face-to-face for a given purpose and desired to do so, they would. We should not find ourselves endlessly comparing a live online experience to the face-to-face version that was never to be in the first place. We are talking about a form of interaction that has a place of its own in the overall landscape of academic communication. So let us be sure we are fair to it regarding its perceived shortcomings when it comes to things we can all agree would be more natural in face-to-face environments.

Understanding the Benefit of Each Nonverbal Cue

To embrace virtual body language is not as daunting as it may seem. We simply need to identify what about certain gestures or facial expressions makes them effective at enhancing the learning environment, and then recognize virtual alternatives that achieve the same instructional outcomes. For example, if eye contact is deemed a crucial immediacy behavior in a given situation, one must determine what specifically it is about eye contact that makes it so important to that particular context. The role eye contact plays might include establishing a connection between student and learner, keeping each learner personally engaged, or providing insight into who comprehends material. Since eye contact, like other forms of body language, can serve different purposes in different situations, this is not necessarily a problem that can be solved globally for all scenarios where one has determined that eye contact is crucial.

One might conclude, for instance, that for a given writing lesson, the role played by eye contact is to help build a connection and sense of trust between instructor and learners, thereby making students more comfortable writing candid autobiographical stories. In that context, suitable virtual facilitation techniques need to be employed to realize a safe environment for sharing. Possibilities might include any number of things, such as having the instructor first use the microphone to share a personal story in her own voice; showing still photographs of each student and the instructor on the screen as they speak to personalize the conversation and build a sense of community; using animated smiling faces to provide instant feedback as a real-time sign that one is following along; or showing live video from the instructor while she listens to learners share their stories, thus allowing the students to see nods of acknowledgment and gauge instructor reaction as they proceed with confidence.

Although it might seem like the most obvious way to communicate nonverbally online, we have saved a more detailed discussion about live video for later in this section, lest we seize on it as a crutch and miss the opportunity to use the full range of nonverbal signals at our disposal. Furthermore, video-based venues will not always be the venue of choice or be a practical option. Used in combination with each other in real time, we have a very powerful set of tools to move, assess, and understand our learners in ways that may be uniquely possible in a synchronous online environment.

Using Emoticons and Abbreviations for Virtual Body Language

Formed by combining the words *emotion* and *icon,* an emoticon is a grouping of typed characters or a small image intended to visually convey a feeling, mood, or emotion. Here are some examples of typed characters that form emoticons:

Emoticon	Sentiment Expressed
:-) or :)	Happiness
:-(or :(	Sadness
;-) or ;(	Wink or sarcasm
:-/	Confused or unsure
:-D	Very happy

In text-based channels of communication, abbreviations or acronyms are also used to quickly share a sentiment or other nonverbal form of behavior. For example:

LOL	Laughing out loud
ROTFL	Rolling on the floor laughing
J/K	Just kidding
TTYL	Talk to you later
BRB	Be right back

The use of emoticons or other text abbreviations is an expedient way of conveying a mood, tone, or shade of meaning in a virtual venue. Although the *New York Herald Tribune* published sideways smiley faces in a print advertisement for the film *Lili* that appeared in 1953 (Wikipedia, retrieved 2005), it was not until almost thirty years later that the first documented instance of the :-) shorthand is believed to have been used online. Seeking a way to compensate for the lack of nonverbal cues in writing and indicate when a message author was joking, Scott Fahlman suggested the sideways smiley emoticon in a 1982 exchange with colleagues on a Carnegie Mellon University online bulletin board (2005). The emoticon "vocabulary" for communicating online has been growing ever since.

Some raise intriguing questions about the effectiveness of emoticons in communicating emotion because "emoticons are clearly intentional uses of nonverbal communication," whereas nonverbal communication is "traditionally and commonly assumed to be unintentional" (Krohn, 2004). Arguably, however, for people who spend substantial time in virtual environments, emoticons may now be a form of self-expression that is as close to a natural and involuntary reflex as the knowing grin or raised eyebrow that may appear ever so subtly on your face as you read this sentence. ;-)

Even if we assume that emoticons actually *are* fraught with intentionality, they still provide a valuable measure of one's attitude or meaning in a way that words alone cannot express. In that regard, they represent an important channel of communication available to us in humanizing and personalizing the synchronous learning realm. If, as Kimberly Carter suggests, computer-mediated communication is "[u]ndeniably . . . developing pseudo-nonverbal protocols that more and more people accept as true representations of actual nonverbal signals" (2003), the question for us as live online instructors is not whether they are intentional, but how to best use them and respond to them in the learning process.

Use Emoticons Liberally

As a general rule, there isn't a constructive criticism so harsh that it cannot be softened by a ;-) or a student response so good that it cannot be followed by enough :-):-). And guilt, an instructor's secret weapon in boosting many students' motivation, is often well-served by a strategically placed :(emoticon.

Solicit Emoticons from Learners

The live online facilitator need not wait for emoticons to be shared by participants but should actively solicit them as a sanctioned and routine part of live online interactions. Specifically asking all learners to submit a smiley face to express comprehension or a frown face to request additional guidance is a highly effective way to "take the virtual pulse" of a group and quickly gauge the atmosphere in a virtual environment.

Some students (or instructors, for that matter) may refrain from using emoticons, perhaps because they consider them unprofessional or are simply not accustomed to their use. Krohn chalks this up to generational distinctions in emoticon comfort levels (2004), yet it would seem from experience that emoticon use increases with actual time spent in virtual environments, regardless of one's age cohort. As people spend more time in virtual environments, they seek out ways of conveying greater subtly to their self-expression. Regardless, the facilitator can create a safe place for emoticons by encouraging and modeling their use.

Use Emoticons Reflexively, and When Listening

Some real-time venues make using emoticons more visually appealing than the typing of punctuation mark combinations on the keyboard. Most instant messengers and chat room tools offer libraries of colorful icons to choose from, and many are even animated to enhance their impact. When someone else is speaking, have your mouse near the emotion indicators. Get in the habit of clicking on an emoticon as a participant is speaking or typing to express your reaction. These real-time cues can provide the encouragement and confidence a learner needs—the equivalent of a nod that says "very good, keep going. . ."—so the student knows whether he or she is treading on safe or fertile ground or whether he or she should reconsider or pause for more live online guidance. This kind of immediacy—instantaneous assessment and feedback in perhaps the most microscopic manner possible online—is unique to synchronous environments and should be utilized to the greatest extent possible.

Using Polls as Proxies for Body Language

Polling is a low-threshold way of involving even the more reticent participants, as it allows for a simple means to take part in and affect the flow of a live online session. Integrated polling tools not only help a facilitator quickly gauge interest, comprehension, and opinions of the subject matter at hand, but they can also be used to appraise more subtle measures of student engagement and understanding: those more akin to the hesitant raising of a hand in a physical classroom.

Pace of Responses

Instructors in face-to-face settings can often judge comprehension as much by the pace at which hands get raised as by the actual answers to the question. This qualitative dimension of assessment is not easily available in asynchronous forums, where the instructor is not present and not able to easily judge things such as the confidence of the learner in his or her responses, or the thought process involved in arriving at an answer. In a live online venue, an observant instructor can glean some rich cues about learner comprehension during the administration of a quick group poll, such as who hesitates, who waits to see how others reply before offering her own opinion, and who waivers and switches his "vote" a few times before settling on an answer (Figure 5.3). This subtlety, if one looks for it and reads it, can improve and personalize online instruction in ways some have not thought was possible online.

Figure 5.3. An Example of How Real-Time Polling Results Provide a Window into Learner Thought Processes, and How That Visual Information Can Be Used in Combination with Text or Audio Communication to Assess Learner Confidence and Understanding.

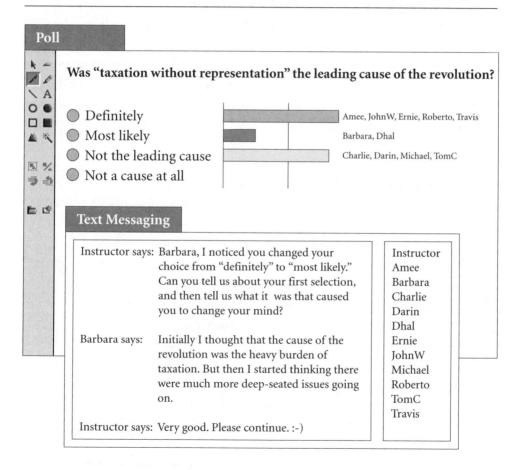

Application of the Results

Live online situations to some extent remove the cover afforded by many asynchronous formats in concealing uncertainty or a weak grasp of important concepts. Tools such as live polling can reveal whether foundational knowledge has telling hairline cracks or reassuring solid supports, and can help determine the needed pace and direction of learning activities going forward. It is important to remember to actually do something with the results of polls conducted in real time. If one asks a series of questions but does not use any of the responses to affect the direction of the learning activity, learners begin to wonder whether their responses matter.

Employing Online Cues to Judge Learner State of Mind

Each interactive face-to-face exchange we have with learners tends to have its own rhythm, pacing, or mood. As educators, we pick up on these intangibles and either reinforce the sense in the room by building on the excitement or try to break the mood with a shift in tactics. When face-to-face, we note things like attentiveness, eye contact, responsiveness, energy, lethargy, and response times. We can tell when a group is "with us" as we lead a learning activity. What kinds of things betray the overall group gestalt in a virtual environment? The following checklist offers a list of some of the more common indicators.

Gauging Group Gestalt in the Virtual Environment

- [ ] When a question is asked, how long does it take before responses are received?
- [ ] How frequently are emoticons being employed?
- [ ] Do you get full and rapid participation when you conduct a poll?
- [ ] How energetic are learners' voices when called upon to use the microphone?
- [ ] Do controversial statements make the interface "light up"?
- [ ] How many people are marked as "idle" or "away" at any given time?
- [ ] Is there ongoing text chat activity while you are speaking?
- [ ] If so, is it related to what you are saying? If tangential, is it still appropriate?
- [ ] When doing whiteboard activities, is everyone participating?
- [ ] Are pauses pregnant or petrifying?
- [ ] How frequently are questions being submitted by participants?
- [ ] How thoughtful are the responses to open-ended questions?
- [ ] Do close-ended questions produce rapid responses?
- [ ] How many people have remained completely inactive and for how long?

- ☐ Is the roster of participant names in flux? Are people dropping off early?
- ☐ If remote desktop sharing is available, are nonrelevant applications viewable on learners' desktops?
- ☐ When a new voice is introduced, such as that of a cofacilitator or student, do people welcome that person in chat or greet him or her with emoticons?
- ☐ Do some emotion indicators stay unchanged for the duration of a session?
- ☐ Are people laughing at your jokes, demonstrated by smiley faces or emotion icons?

Live online environments should help take the guesswork out of knowing how learners are responding to the learning activities at hand. Remember, one should always wonder, but never be left wondering, whether learners are on track.

Using Video for Virtual Body Language

For some, using live video is the most obvious answer to conveying virtual body language and a sense of immediacy. Used well and appropriately, live video can deliver a very powerful and human experience. With video increasingly available in synchronous venues and steadily improving in quality as bandwidth to the desktop gets better, we will undoubtedly continue to see more live motion in online learning venues.

Contemplating the use of live video in an online session still brings with it a range of considerations that need to be weighed against the intended learning objectives. For example:

- Will everyone have the technical requirements and bandwidth to see it?
- Will those who cannot technically or otherwise see the live video still be able to benefit from the experience (for example, through audio, closed captioning, or other means)?
- Will the motion enhance or distract from the learning objectives?
- Will the lighting and other ambient factors in a nonstudio environment be acceptable?
- Will some participants or instructors be reluctant to use video themselves, prizing the visual anonymity or shielding that is afforded by online settings?
- Will the impact of using the video be worth the effort it may take to technically prepare for a video-based session?

If due consideration is given and video is warranted and can be supported, an excellent primary or auxiliary channel for conveying nonverbal communication is available. Exhibit 5.2 offers some practical tips for using video successfully.

RELY ON OTHERS: YOU ARE NOT ALONE

Live online facilitation need not be done solo. In fact, there are many great reasons to consider sharing the virtual podium with a cofacilitator when leading an online session, especially when interacting with larger sized groups of participants. Whether one plans in advance to work with a cohost or decides spontaneously during an event to promote one of the participants to a leading role, collaborative facilitation can be a worthwhile enterprise on many levels.

A Cofacilitator by Any Other Name

There are many ways to consider those who share live online facilitation responsibilities with us, such as coteachers, cofacilitators, teaching assistants, producers, moderators, panelists, cohosts, guest hosts, guest experts, student teachers, technical assistants, apprentices, emcees, sidekicks, opening acts, or sous-chefs. Regardless of the vocabulary we use, those we enlist to help facilitate a live online session can be an indispensable resource to both instructor and learners.

Benefits to Instructors and Learners of Team Teaching Live Online

In reflecting on their experiences with university coteaching, Greg Conderman and Bonnie McCarty have suggested that a collaborative approach to facilitating provides "unique instructional benefits for our students as well as powerful professional benefits for ourselves" (2003). Jack Hourcade and Jeanne Bauwens have elucidated some of these benefits in suggesting that cooperative teaching "allows educators to pool their individual strengths and talents to enhance the learning of all students in an instructionally more powerful environment. It allows students to interact with a variety of educators who bring differing styles, personalities, and skills to the learning environment" (2001, p. 247). Although they were not specifically referring to live online contexts, their conclusions about cofacilitation are certainly applicable to the realm of synchronous instruction.

From an instructor's perspective, having a counterpart online during a synchronous session

Exhibit 5.2. Tips for Using Video Successfully.

Here are some quick tips for improving the quality of synchronous sessions for which live video has been selected as a communication option.

- *Focus on eye contact: look directly into the camera.* The impact on the learner can be quite striking when the person behind the camera takes a page out of a television anchor's playbook and makes the audience feel as though she is looking right at them. If one frequently looks elsewhere, it can distract viewers. It may seem a bit odd at first, but one's eyes need to be focused as much as possible on the camera lens, as a proxy for the learner. This takes some practice, but is like riding a bike; once you get the hang of it, you won't forget.

- *Every moment on video matters. Especially the first ones.* If a picture says a thousand words, a *moving* one at thirty frames per second says at least that much every thirtieth of a second. Research tells us that a "thin slice of nonverbal" behavior before a course begins (for example, a silent video clip of an instructor of under thirty seconds in duration) is enough for learners to make accurate predictions about that teacher's ultimate end-of-semester student evaluations (Ambady and Rosenthal, 1993). If you decide to use video, be aware of what messages your nonverbal behaviors are sending to your learners. It is hard to have a second chance to make a first impression.

- *Position the camera so you can see learner feedback as it comes in.* Position the camera so it is in front of the area of your screen where participants' video is displayed (in a multiway video environment) or in front of the area of the interface where learner input (such as text or poll responses) appears. That way, you can look directly into the camera and still notice immediately when learners are responding to you.

- *Use video strategically. It need not be all or nothing.* Consider using video for certain segments of a live online session rather than for an entire class. Turn video on at the outset, for example, and then return to it later in a session to put stronger emphasis on concluding thoughts. Video can have its greatest impact when used with discretion. If used all the time, viewers will lose interest and tune it out. Important nonverbal cues will be lost among gratuitous ones. If turned on strategically, and for good reasons, video is less likely to lose its oomph.

- *Authentic surroundings, good lighting, engaging props.* Although some instructors will opt for a solid backdrop, there is nothing wrong with exposing your actual surroundings. It builds a sense of closeness when people see you in your authentic environment—especially when that environment enhances your credibility (for example, don't hide the brain in the jar on your desk during your biology lesson). Be mindful of good lighting or you can wind up wasting bandwidth if no one can see you.

- *Listening on video can be at least as important as speaking on video.* When Neale Godfrey teachers her financial literacy classes live online, more than half of her time on camera is spent actively listening and visually reassuring learners as they speak. Let students see you nod, smile, or otherwise react as they speak.

- *Don't forget you're on camera.* It's easy to forget when you are alone in a physical room that people are watching you. But it can be embarrassing, for obvious reasons, when you do. Try not to forget.

- Allows responsibility for different aspects of the lesson content to be shared during a live session
- Permits one person to focus on content while the other takes on technical functions and support
- Provides a peer with whom one can prepare before and reflect after a live online experience
- Allows one facilitator to attend to participant concerns—perhaps in an auxiliary communication channel—while the other facilitator leads a primary activity
- Enables one person to work in the background adjusting or creating the next set of live activities based on learner contributions shared earlier in a session
- Gives the session leaders the opportunity to model interactivity through dialogue, cross-questioning, and banter and to stimulate participation among learners

Looking at things from the vantage point of a participant in a synchronous setting, the presence of more than one facilitator online

- Offers multiple voices and engaging dynamics that keep things lively
- Provides multiple perspectives and approaches to the topic at hand
- Improves the instructor-to-student ratio and increases the likelihood of participants having direct interaction with a session leader, especially during larger group sessions
- Allows more than one communication channel to be fully utilized and monitored at the same time (such as text and audio), offering more communication options suited to different learning styles
- Furnishes a responsive outlet for technical or logistical questions that arise during a live activity, and allows certain topics to be taken out of the public spaces so as not to distract other learners from a primary activity

Exhibit 5.3 offers examples of some of the special "sidekick" roles that others can play in assisting with the facilitation of live online activities.

USE THE SYNCHRONOUS DASHBOARD

In many synchronous venues—especially those of virtual classrooms, meeting rooms, interactive Webcasts, or sophisticated chat rooms—the facilitator view of

Exhibit 5.3. Six Significant Sidekick Roles
in the Synchronous Environment.

Voice of the Web

The "Voice of the Web" (or VOW) keeps a finger on the pulse of online participants and conveys it to the facilitator. He or she looks for common threads appearing in the chat room, reports on poll results, summarizes sidebar discussions, and chimes in periodically to give voice to a collective Web-based audience. The VOW ensures that all real-time contributions are recognized and attempts to keep all channels of communication connected to one another so that they don't diverge or devolve into unrelated conversations. The VOW can be designated in advance or selected on the fly from among participants.

Producer

The "producer" turns a live learning event into a true production. He or she works with the facilitator to prepare the session and then keeps an eye on everything during its live delivery: from welcoming participants as they arrive to ensuring that things begin and end on time to working behind the scenes to orchestrate the display of visuals and media to complement the facilitator's substantive activity. The producer often has a flare for making learning feel like theater, but also is quite dexterous when it comes to manipulating technology. Part stage manager, part co-host, the producer role can sometimes overlap with technical support and VOW functions, as the producer does it all to ensure everyone's time together is well spent and worthy of the live environment.

Designated Skeptic

The "designated skeptic" can be chosen on the fly by a facilitator to play a devil's advocate role throughout a live session or a specific learning activity. As the event proceeds, the skeptic is urged to use available tools to voice disagreement, confusion, or questions. Without the kind of nonverbal cues to which many are accustomed in a physical space, it can sometimes be hard to know when learners are rolling their eyes, sighing, or reacting in disbelief. It is the sanctioned job of the designated skeptic to voice a contrarian's attitude, to which the instructor can respond or direct others to do so. It is better to have someone doing the sighing publicly and without recourse than to not know when it might be happening and risk losing contingents of the group.

Co-host or Guest Expert

A "co-host" helps the facilitator model substantive discussion on the given topic for students. The co-host also complements the facilitator by offering banter that builds a sense of community and provides instant interactivity and a built-in change of voice and pace. A "guest expert" provides a dose of authenticity regarding the subject matter. Synchronous

(Continued)

Exhibit 5.3. Continued.

online venues can support guests logging in from anywhere in the world, and learners can interact with those putting theory into practice. Co-hosts are also helpful in monitoring breakout rooms when those are put to use for concurrent exercises.

Technical Support Assistant

A designated "technical support assistant" can field all matters related to the workings (or nonworkings) of the synchronous venue so that a facilitator can focus on the learning activities at hand during the live event. A facilitator should know a "top three" list of most frequent technical issues if in a pinch, but full-blown technical support during a live event should be placed in the capable hands of a technical support assistant.

Studio Audience

A "studio audience" can be one, a small handful, or many people (learners or cofacilitators) who are present at the same location as the main facilitator. Sitting near the facilitator, the studio audience provides instant nonverbal, visual, and auditory feedback that can keep a facilitator on task and give remote learners an extra voice to represent them.

the interface often feels somewhat like the dashboard of a car. In more complex systems, it can even look like an airplane cockpit. Participant activity indicators, bandwidth meters, chat rooms, private messaging areas, media loading progress gauges, slide lists, breakout room controls, question queues, poll result displays— taken as a whole, all of these "gizmos" constitute an instructor's console that can help manage the flow of an educational activity and assist in moving a group of people from a point A to a point B, or a point X, for that matter.

Leading Live Online Learning: Driving a Car

In some respects, leading live online sessions can be much like driving a car. Anyone who has progressed from being a beginning driver to a regular behind the wheel of an automobile knows that at some point one achieves a comfort level where the experience becomes second nature. Yes, there are dials and gauges always in motion, but we learn quickly with experience how to glance from time to time or use our peripheral vision to take in these cues without becoming obsessive about studying them at every moment.

When drivers reach a certain level of comfort, they will often have some bewildering moments when they find they got from point A to point B safely, but have little recollection of what they actually *did* with the car's controls to get there. Arguably, this is a good metaphor for live online facilitation. We don't want to be prisoners of the technology, being preoccupied with the operation of bells and whistles while losing focus on where we are headed, or on our passengers.

Integrating Learner Feedback Seamlessly

Perhaps out of nervousness with the new medium or habit from their approach in the physical realm, many instructors, when beginning to conduct live online activities, will pay little or no attention to instructor console indicators. They fall into a "lecture mode" in which they miss important cues and questions that come in from participants. They may approach the last few moments of a live session and only just begin to review the feedback that has accumulated. However, as with driving a car, that's too long to go without taking note of what the dashboard is telling us. As already discussed, the live online realm is usually not the right place for lecturing. Lectures, if needed, can be recorded and posted asynchronously for review at the convenience of the learner. One of the main reasons to do something live is for the immediacy and ability to react to our learners and colleagues in real time. For this reason, "cruise control" is a part of the dashboard metaphor that should rarely have a place in synchronous settings.

What follows are some facilitation tips regarding the use of the synchronous dashboard to be responsive to learners, while keeping the session moving in the right direction. Every instructor's style and the purpose of every live session will be different; the guidelines presented here are just suggestions to help put the tools to good use while staying focused on the learning taking place.

Note Changes or Flickers

When facilitating a session be alert to *changes* in the interface, such as the arrival of new chat messages or virtual hands being raised. With experience, one gets attuned to the various inputs as *flickers* on the screen, which attract attention. Exhibit 5.4 offers some example phrases to help you integrate those flickers into the overall flow of a live session.

Set Ground Rules to Establish a Baseline

Set expectations or ground rules upfront with your participants about when and how they should share questions and comments throughout the session. That way,

Exhibit 5.4. Example Phrases Illustrating How to Naturally Integrate Dashboard Feedback into the Flow of a Live Session.

This exhibit contains a few examples of phrases that illustrate how a facilitator can respond to various cues and feedback that come in through a synchronous interface while maintaining the appropriate flow of the session and a sense among learners that their presence matters.

- "I see that there are several virtual hands raised. I am just going to finish reviewing this diagram, and I will get to them in just a moment."

- "Jim has posted a good question in the chat area, and I see a few of you have begun to respond. It is clearly a great discussion topic. Since we have a few other topics to discuss today, Jim, I'd like to ask you to post your question in the discussion board in our online course area where others can share their feedback throughout the week. We'll start next week's live session with a summary from Jim of what he has learned from all of your feedback in the threaded forum."

- "I am going to pause for a minute here to catch up on all of the messages I see posted. Let me just ask you not to post anything new for the next moment as I review all of your great comments."

- "A few people are smiling [using the emoticons], which is great. We'll find out in a moment why the rest of you aren't."

- "And so there are several categories of magic: stage, parlor, and—as I see Lizzie has just suggested in the chat area—escape artistry. Lizzie, I know you did this week's paper on Houdini. Can you tell us a little bit about. . . ."

- "Howard, I just want to let you know that I saw your question from earlier. I think the activity that Bill has planned for his student project will address that, so let's hold off on that for now."

- "Rick and Phoebe—earlier I thought I saw you submit questions, but I must admit I was a bit carried away with my explanation. Would you please ask them again?"

- "As I was talking, I noticed several mentions in the chat area about whether this or that will be on the final. The short answer is 'yes.'"

- "That's why ionic bonds display these characteristics. [Martina raises a virtual hand.] In our virtual lab a little earlier, we were examining covalent bonds. Who can tell me how these bonds are different? Martina, you had your hand raised before I asked the question. Go ahead and answer my question, and then I'll answer yours." [Instructor clicks smiley emoticon and gives microphone to Martina.]

- "And that's why zebras have stripes. [Emoticons start blinking with smiley faces.] I see a number of you smiling. I think you all suspect I was joking, but no, in fact, that *is* my evolutionary theory as to why zebras have stripes."

when new inputs appear, you will have a quicker idea of what they are and how to respond to them. For example, let learners know that they should use their virtual hand-raise button to get your attention if they have a pressing question even while you are speaking. When a hand goes up, you can assume the reason is worthy of interruption.

Acknowledge the Existence of Feedback

Acknowledging the presence of feedback is as at least as important as providing a substantive response to it. Sometimes it is impossible to respond to every individual input during a session, or for any number of reasons, you may want to table certain questions or avoid them altogether. You can acknowledge input without necessarily responding to it immediately. Exhibit 5.4 includes some examples of phrases that you might use to convey a sense of your responsiveness as a facilitator, without losing your train of thought or straying too far from your time frame or agenda.

BE PREPARED AND MANAGE CRISES

One of the best aspects of synchronous settings is the unanticipated learning that can happen when people interact in real time without a script. Being prepared allows you to better handle the good, yet unpredictable, kinds of interaction that can emerge—such as constructive tangents or unplanned virtual field trips—but it also improves your chances of managing unforeseen technical or logistical issues that can arise. Facilitating live online learning is much like delivering a live theater performance in that every audience is different, anything can happen, and the show must go on.

Preparing for Spontaneity and Learning Live Online

Some synchronous activities are spontaneous by nature, such as unannounced exchanges with a student or colleague via instant messenger, whereas others are planned well in advance, such as an online seminar or class. Clearly, the stakes are higher with the scheduled live interactions, as they often involve a group of people all of whom have arranged their lives to be online together at the same time, and who bring with them an expectation that the person who is leading the meeting will ensure the time is worth their while. Impromptu live interaction often carries somewhat less in the way of expectations, in that it is a just-in-time form of outreach. I will focus here on preparing for those synchronous activities about which we have some advance warning and lead time to prepare.

But there can be *too much* preparation. One does not want to be prepared to the point that learners feel as though a live session was scripted and that every possible twist and turn was predetermined—or that there were no twists and turns. This is as true online as it is when teaching face-to-face. Though a good facilitator has a plan, he or she still manages to make every participant feel that he or she has contributed to and constructed the course of events and the ultimate outcome.

Chat Room Preparation

Each instructor will have his or her own preference when it comes to using text-based chat rooms for formal instructional activities, versus more ad hoc drop-in sessions with no prescribed agenda. Some find typing in real time cumbersome and prefer a more full-featured virtual classroom with audio capabilities. Others appreciate the simplicity and low technology barriers to participation in chat room venues, and the fact that these text-based tools provide a small buffer or window of time in between messages, allowing one to compose a thought and review it briefly before sharing it with others.

Although one does not want to script an entire chat room session, it is often possible to prepare "anchor points" in advance that will ease the typing burden on the facilitator during the actual event while keeping the chat activity on track. These anchors, which can then be copied and pasted into the chat room, might include things like

- A series of precomposed prompt questions to stimulate and guide discussion
- Selected quotes from course readings to provide a common basis for dialogue
- Web links to online course materials for review together online
- Excerpts from asynchronous student discussions in a course Web site for continuity and elaboration
- Selections from work submitted by students to initiate peer analysis

It can also be useful to have transcripts from prior chat room sessions on hand for comparison and copying and pasting. For example, an instructor might say something like this during a live chat:

How does this new information we just learned affect the conclusions we drew in our chat last week? This comment from Amanda from our last live session summed up our analysis quite well: [instructor pastes a chat transcript excerpt from Amanda from the prior week's live chat]. Would any of you change your mind about this based on what we learned today?

It is often possible to anticipate frequently asked questions that might arise. For this purpose, one can prepare a set of answers or responses that can either be pasted into the chat should the questions be asked or posted on the course Web site before or after the chat so that time spent live online can be used for constructing new knowledge.

Virtual Classroom and Interactive Webcast Preparation

In addition to preparing a specific instructional plan and any accompanying resources for a live online virtual classroom or interactive Webcast session, facilitators might also consider undertaking a few other tasks in advance that may give them more confidence and freedom if a session takes unexpected turns. The following are some tips for preparing for sessions in these venues.

Have More Content on Hand Than You Need

Having more content on hand than is needed allows you the freedom to adjust the live session on the fly based on learner interest, questions, or requests.

Use Technical Slides

It is not always possible to have someone on hand to provide technical support. Having a few basic technical visuals at your disposal that depict screenshots with solutions to the more common technical problems can help you in a pinch when technical support is unavailable.

Keep Digital Photos of Learners or Panelists on Hand

It is a nice practice, when feasible, to have headshots of each of your learners or panelists available during a live session. Bringing up a photograph of someone who is speaking personalizes the environment and serves as an impromptu tactic to keeping learners engaged when there are no obvious visuals to display, such as during a question-and-answer period or meaningful digression.

Access Visuals from Previous Live Sessions

Sometimes points made in prior classes resurface in future lessons; having easy access to the content of prior live classes ensures continuity, and allows one to respond in real time to unanticipated questions that build on prior learning experiences. Showing actual student work from prior sessions helps create a sense of pride and accountability, thus reassuring students that contributions are not forgotten.

Use Whiteboard Screen Templates

Grid templates divided into boxes and labeled with the name of each learner can be useful when you decide at a moment's notice to conduct a whiteboard activity and want each participant to have a discrete space to share his or her work or reflections.

Have Supporting Materials on Hand

It is also useful to have at your virtual fingertips things such as the course syllabus, reading materials, recent assignments, or the online course site itself so that these items can be shared or integrated within the discussion as the need arises.

One-on-One Sessions

One-on-one live online sessions are highly individualized to the needs of the learner and are often highly spontaneous. The kind of general preparation suggested for facilitating these two-person synchronous scenarios will vary significantly depending on the context, but it is not that dissimilar from work one would do before a virtual classroom meeting, or in an offline tutoring environment, for that matter. A virtual tutoring checklist might include

- A visual or slide library of sample exercises or questions
- The review and loading of common slides used by other tutors in your institution
- Previous work completed by the student from prior live sessions or submitted asynchronously

Preparing for the Worst: When Technical Crises Strike, Live Online

Learning experiences in face-to-face settings are not immune to technical problems, but when everyone is gathered in the same physical location there is at least a common understanding of the nature of the difficulty encountered. For example, if the bulb in a slide projector suddenly goes out during a lesson, everyone in the classroom has a pretty immediate grasp of the situation, and the instructor can directly communicate contingency plans or adjust accordingly. By contrast, in a real-time online setting, there is not always the luxury of an immediate and shared perception of the cause of any technical mishaps that may transpire. This uncertainty and lack of connection—no matter how briefly it may last—can cause a sense of isolation and panic to set in.

Table 5.2 offers a series of key steps that facilitators of live online sessions can take to prevent technical glitches from taking center stage during synchronous events.

Table 5.2. Preventing Technical Issues from Hijacking a Live Online Learning Opportunity.

Days Before a Live Session

Login at least a few days early.	Access and test the virtual venue from the computer and Web connection you intend to use at least several days before your live session to ensure enough time to seek support should anything not be working properly.
Send a technical configuration link to all participants.	Many synchronous platforms have a configuration area or "pre-flight" link that automatically checks a computer's ability to connect to a live session. Direct all learners to this link before their first time participating live online.
Orchestrate tech "drop-in" times for first-time participants.	For a course or seminar that will include regularly scheduled live sessions, you might consider scheduling some "drop-in" times before the first substantive session. These can be optional and give learners a chance to get acclimated to the virtual venue, while also ensuring that they have no major technical issues. It also allows the instructor to begin to build a sense of community and get comfortable with a live group in a low-stakes setting without a formal lesson plan or agenda.

(Continued)

Table 5.2. Continued.

Prepare a back-up plan.	Do you have access to a second computer that can be logged in near you in case your primary computer crashes during the event? What will you do if you lose your Internet connection during the live session? Is there someone you can call who can be online to assist, take over, or let participants know what has happened? Considering where you can achieve redundancy or have contingency plans is always wise. The lower the stakes of the session, and the longer the track record you have with a given venue and computer, the less concern you will have for back-up plans, but it is best not to be complacent when it comes to preparedness. Technical snafus bite when you least expect them.
Right Before a Live Session	
Login several minutes early.	Showing up just as your live session begins does not give you much time to deal with unexpected technical issues that can crop up, even if you tested your computer the day before. Once logged in safely, you can test major functions, such as audio or video tools, prep the virtual venue for the session, or multitask before learners arrive.
Reboot your computer.	If you can, use a computer you know and trust. Either way, give the computer a fresh start before you begin; turn it off and reboot it. Close any unnecessary applications; not only does this maximize computer resources available, it limits distractions.
Prepare your physical surroundings.	Assess your physical space and see how you can prepare it for maximum comfort and minimum distractions. If you are in a busy office area close the door or post a "Do Not Disturb" sign. Let your colleagues, family, or friends know before you begin that you will be indisposed for the next hour or so. Have a beverage of choice nearby and even some snacks. Some instructors like to keep paper nearby to take notes. It can be a great way to stay focused on what learners contribute or to jot down thoughts that occur to you to address later.

Print materials for reference and backup.	It is not a bad idea to print a hard copy of slides or other visuals. This not only gives you something from which to work should your own computer have problems, but it also provides an easy way to jot down notes on areas of student concern as you proceed.
Peruse your course Web site, and take a quick peek at e-mail.	Look at your e-mail and peruse the interactive areas of your course Web site for last-minute posts or questions from learners. This will allow you to connect the live experience with even the most recent asynchronous discussions. Students are often very impressed with the instructor and proud of themselves when the comments, assignments, or projects they share in discussion boards or digital drop boxes are recognized live online. The real-time acknowledgment reminds them that you are paying attention to their efforts across the continuum of channels through which they can contribute. It also helps keep learners motivated and at their best.
Greet your learners. Warm them up and get them ready to learn.	When you are logged in and ready early, you can be a calm or energetic presence welcoming learners as they arrive. This also provides the opportunity to have brief but warm conversations with individuals or small groups of learners, providing individualized attention and reinforcement that positively affects motivation.

During a Live Session

Set technical ground rules at the outset.	To minimize unnecessary disruptions, remind learners where to direct questions of a technical nature if they should arise. As a general rule, technical issues should be sent privately to a designated support person and not sent in public channels. Reinforce that it may not be possible to resolve individual tech problems during the live session, and that transcripts or recordings will be available. Do not take time away from the session to rescue one person while jeopardizing the good will of all.
Assess how widespread a problem seems to be.	There are many points of possible failure in a distributed synchronous learning environment. When signs of a technical issue emerge it is helpful to assess whether it

(Continued)

Table 5.2. Continued.

	is an individual issue or something more global. If a problem is localized to just one participant, he or she can resort to the help procedures you have outlined, and you can keep focused on the substantive learning matters at hand.
Be transparent. Remain calm.	If you are having a problem that is interfering with your ability to facilitate, it is usually better to acknowledge it, calmly ask for a brief moment to resolve it, or talk your way through it aloud.
Remain in control.	It is easy to get thrown off balance when a technical issue takes you by surprise and causes you to lose your footing. Many technical issues get resolved quickly. Once you have jumped over the hurdle, take a deep breath, and help reinflate the bubble of concentration for you and your learners.
Know when to reschedule.	Sometimes, a technical problem affecting all or a substantial number of people cannot be resolved during the live session time. It is important to know when to give up, reschedule, or defer dialogue to other means, such as another real-time venue, a discussion board, or even the phone.
Nip "tech talk" in the bud. Refocus the dialogue.	If you see technical cross-talk invading the public communication channels that are not serving the common good or the matters at hand, don't hesitate to jump in and ask for such dialogue to be halted or saved for later. There are times when "tech talk" is appropriate, but otherwise this kind of exchange can be disruptive.
Step back and remember the ultimate goal.	If during a session, a particular tool is not working properly but other aspects of the environment are fine, take a step back and remind yourself of the ultimate goal—which rarely is simply to use a particular tool. The goal is to achieve a particular learning outcome. Look around you and think about what else can be done to make good use of everyone's time. Be creative.

Real-Time Online Learning Activities

The effectiveness of a good facilitator in a real-time, online environment is supported and enhanced by the integration of well-designed, meaningful learning activities. Just as an empty, physical classroom can support a wide array of instructional options, a virtual classroom is a veritable blank canvas for conducting activities that foster collaboration, interaction, and learning. With so many possibilities, it is important to focus in upon appropriate approaches for a given situation that will hold up the instructor's end of the "synchronous compact"—his or her implicit responsibility to make the best use of all participants' time together, live online.

Intended as a set of sample approaches to jumpstart the design of effective real-time learning activities, rather than a comprehensive listing, each activity that follows constitutes a template that can be applied or adapted to virtually any subject matter being explored in a live online environment. In addition to a brief overview and suggested tools or venues for each approach, each template offers discipline-specific examples, variations, facilitation tips, and suggestions for embedding the live experience into a broader online learning context, including asynchronous coursework.

MAGNETIC BRAINSTORMS

The entire group of participants, responding in real time to a prompt question from the facilitator, concurrently posts words or brief phrases on a virtual whiteboard. After the words emerge on the screen, they are moved around like refrigerator magnets and categorized, ordered, or assembled by a designated person or a small subset of the group, according to facilitator instructions.

Purpose

This activity engages the full group by soliciting concurrent contributions from everyone while also putting one or two people in the spotlight to synthesize or organize peer input. Engagement levels are usually very high during Magnetic Brainstorms, as each participant tracks how his or her own contribution is perceived and manipulated by the group. Participants also tend to be empathetic and give their undivided attention to their peers; they think about how they would have handled the same task if they had been put in the spotlight.

- Constructs learning experience of participants together
- Collects input quickly and simultaneously from all learners
- Assures that everyone's contributions are used in the lesson; no one is left out
- Builds sense of community
- Provides opportunity to assess student confidence, knowledge, and creativity on the fly
- Offers a fun and engaging interlude on which to sustain or build learning momentum

Suitable Venues
- Virtual classroom
- Virtual meeting room or virtual office
- Adaptable to virtual reference desk for tutoring purposes

Tools Used

- Multi-user, object-oriented whiteboard
- Two-way audio (VoIP or phone) recommended

Example Activity

In this example, the Magnetic Brainstorm approach is used for the collaborative generation of poetry with words supplied by the whole group (Figure 6.1).

Figure 6.1. Magnetic Brainstorm.

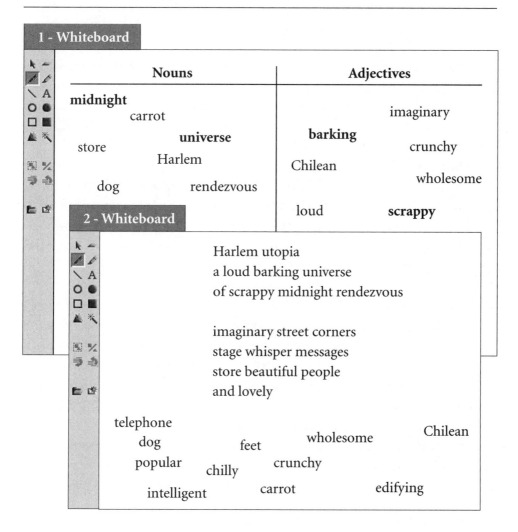

1. *Brainstorm:* The instructor draws a line to divide a blank virtual white-board screen, and asks all participants to type in a noun on one side of the screen and an adjective on the other. The instructor allows a few seconds for the whiteboard to fill up with words and provides some vocal encouragement as warranted. After a virtual "pens down" the instructor turns off the whiteboard text tools for all participants.

2. *Magnetize:* Next, the instructor asks for a volunteer or designates one or two participants to click and drag the words around to form a poem, and provides more specific guidance as needed. Volunteers are asked to use the audio tool available to think out loud and share their thought process with the whole group.

3. *Debrief:* The instructor designates a new volunteer to read the finished work aloud to the group. After saluting the volunteers for their performance and reminding all learners that this poem originated from all of their contributions, the instructor debriefs learners to analyze the final work or performance according to given criteria, or reflect on the overall process or poetic devices used.

Facilitation Tips

Let the participants drive this activity. Consider yourself a cheerleader or coach, providing enthusiasm and only as much instruction as needed to get the full group involved. This can be used as an introductory activity for a given live session as a way of getting the group in a participatory and collaborative mindset while also introducing a theme of relevance to the session.

Other Applications

The example above is a construction exercise, where words are assembled to form a poem. This approach can be adapted to other applications such as storytelling or writing. Categorization, ordering, and other brainstorming applications are also very suitable for this approach. For example, the facilitator in an organizational behavior class asks participants to supply words or phrases that describe *attributes of a good leader,* which are then organized on screen by whether they reflect traits that are innate or can be learned. In yet another example, the original submissions solicited might be historical events, and the volunteer might be asked to move them around, ordering or ranking them to reflect their significance.

Variations on This Activity

Designate a Commentator. One engaging variation on this activity is to designate a second volunteer to offer running commentary via audio as the initial volunteer is moving the words around the screen. This commentator may be likened to a television sports announcer, who narrates what he or she sees unfolding on the screen. The commentator can be invited to be opinionated, affecting the word placement, or to merely be descriptive. This twist to the Magnetic Brainstorm pulls more learners into the process.

Tag Team. While the words are being moved around on the screen, ask the volunteer to hand the whiteboard controls over to a different participant to continue the exercise.

Guest Expert. Invite a guest expert in to be the person doing the ordering or constructing or to be the commentator. In the case of the poetry example, a guest poet adds some authenticity to the activity, and learners are able to get inside the mind of an accomplished person in the field while their own words become the subject of his work.

Within a Broader Online Learning Context

The Magnetic Brainstorm activity can provide segues in and out of other synchronous exercises and can also be used to connect or build upon asynchronous course work completed by learners. Ideas might be collected at the beginning of a live lesson on the whiteboard. A lesson or other activity might ensue, and then the facilitator can return to the original whiteboard and ask the volunteer—based on the intervening discussion—to arrange the student submissions accordingly.

In the context of an overall online course, one might prearrange the whiteboard to include submissions from a threaded discussion forum. When students arrive, they revisit their contributions in real time according to a new set of instructions. This can keep learners on their toes when completing their asynchronous work, setting the precedent that any contribution—even one completed independently—can later take the spotlight during live group activities.

STONE SOUP

Learners move into breakout room areas according to individual responses to a poll question. While in smaller groups, participants work together on a common project, contributing ideas, solving a problem, or completing a task. After a certain period, the facilitator returns all participants to the main area, where select group results are summarized, showcased, discussed, rated, compared, or used as the basis for a subsequent lesson or activity.

The Stone Soup type of activity gets its name from a fable of the same in which a group of hungry travelers come upon a village during hard times and finds that none of the residents are willing to share their food. After the hungry travelers put a stone in a pot of water and boil it in the town square, the villagers emerge with interest and begin to contribute ingredients to what becomes a communal soup that is far tastier than mere stone-steeped water. In Stone Soup synchronous activities, the facilitator starts groups of learners with a simple nugget of information, directions, and a problem or image, and each learner brings something to the table to foster a meaningful group discussion or process that can then be shared with the full class after it has had some time to "cook."

Purpose

This activity groups learners—often by ability, perspective, or interest—and actively engages them in collaborative, concurrent discussion and project-based or problem-solving work with peers. It allows the instructor to cover more ground than would be possible if all learners were assembled in one room, virtual or otherwise. In the course of wrapping up Stone Soup activities, learners share and compare the results of their group work, learning from each other about different approaches to the same problem or about new topics entirely.

- Increases level of individual participation through small group collaboration
- Covers greater amount of material through concurrent activities
- Improves engagement by allowing learners to choose or influence their own path
- Groups learners with similar abilities so that more advanced learners are sufficiently challenged while less advanced ones do not feel out of their element
- Mixes learners of varying competencies together to foster peer mentoring or coaching
- Builds a sense of community and fosters collaboration through group work

- Creates a sense of building toward something by not letting learners know what will happen after they leave their breakout rooms, and hence keeps engagement levels high

Suitable Venues

- Virtual classroom
- Virtual meeting room or virtual office
- Chat room
- Multi-user virtual environment (MUVE)

Tools Used

- Breakout rooms or equivalent multichannel platform
- Nonanonymous polling
- Slide or image showing tool
- Public text messaging
- Two-way audio (VoIP or phone) recommended
- Whiteboard recommended

Example Activity

This example uses the fable for which the activity itself is named as the "stone" to seed discussion in each breakout room. The particular activity might be used in any number of disciplines to emphasize themes related to collaboration, sharing, oral traditions, or storytelling.

1. *Poll and divide the group*: The facilitator uses the polling feature to find out who in the group is familiar with the story "Stone Soup." Learners are then instructed that they will be split into breakout rooms according to their poll responses, where they will see a book cover illustration depicting the story "Stone Soup." Each room's goal is to collaborate to arrive at a definitive version of the story and its concluding moral. The facilitator reminds participants that they may not use any outside resources, such as Web sites, to assist in the task. At this point, those who indicated "yes" are moved into one breakout room, and those who voted "no"

are moved into a separate breakout room. For particularly large groups, multiple rooms for each group can be used.

2.   *Allow groups to collaborate*: Participants enter their respective rooms, see the book cover graphic waiting for them on their screens, and begin to use the text chat, audio, or video tools available to them to discuss and collaborate. Learners may also use the whiteboard to annotate the image or to take notes on the screen.

3.   *Reunite the groups, share, and debrief*: After a suitable time, the groups are reunited in the main room, where the facilitator asks a representative of each team to present the synopsis and moral of the story. The group unfamiliar with the story is asked to go first, both for effect (the stories can often be quite humorous) and so as not to be unduly influenced by first hearing the other group's rendition. After both groups share, the facilitator debriefs with learners about the experience.

Facilitation Tips

The instructor can move between rooms to quietly assess progress and student performance, or stay in one room and have a teaching assistant monitor the other. The exact time spent in breakout rooms need not be fixed or predetermined.

Other Applications

The Stone Soup template can be used for an array of learning objectives and subject matter areas. Some possibilities include

- Provide a case study or set of facts in each room, and ask each group to decide what they would do in each situation. Then compare or contrast the decisions made in each room.
- Set up each breakout room with a virtual lab simulation and a different set of variables. Learners in each room conduct the lab together and then compare results with other groups in the main room.
- Provide a series of movable images on the whiteboard in each room and instruct groups to work together to put the images in order. This might include arranging the steps in a technical process or in software design, for example.
- Conduct a storytelling exercise similar to the one above, but have learners do it in a foreign language.
- Provide a math problem on the whiteboard in each room and ask learners to collaborate on a solution via a specified method, showing their work on the

whiteboard. In the main room, each group walks through how they solved the problem by the approach assigned to them.

- Use the initial poll to gauge an opinion on an important issue, and then create heterogeneous groups so that discussion includes a diversity of opinions and is fertile for debate.

Variations on This Activity

Obstacle Course. Keep the content, problem, or topic in each breakout room the same, and rotate groups from room to room, like a group obstacle course, addressing the task they find in each room. Debrief as a full group after a few rotations and compare group approaches to each task.

Black Box. Provide no instruction before sending learners to the breakout rooms or once they arrive in their respective areas. Simply provide a primary source, chart, photograph, diagram, or other digital object and see how learners react to it and what kind of discussion it generates. Controversial images or tables reflecting what look like incongruous trends are good ways to spark discussion and can help learners discuss discipline-specific topics in a self-directed way with peers.

Within a Broader Online Learning Context

Use Stone Soup exercises to introduce asynchronous course materials in a safe team-oriented manner. For example, place brief selections from class readings in each breakout room. Learners meet and discuss the excerpt so all have a good grasp of the issue before they are sent out for the week to tackle the rest of the readings on their own. Another Stone Soup "seed" might be selected student work from an online course, posted in each room as the basis for group discussion.

SOLO FISHBOWLS

Learners are given a portion of a shared workspace or whiteboard where they work independently to respond to a problem or complete a task while in the virtual presence of a small group of peers, whose work they also see. The facilitator peruses all student work in progress in real time, and continues to provide subsequent instructions or guidance even as learners work in their own "fishbowl" to complete the assignment. Since participants are sharing a visual workspace with a small subset of peers, they enjoy the safety of company that can help them decide whether they are on the right track, or they can choose to take a very different tack with their own response than those they see others taking.

Purpose

The Solo Fishbowl allows learners to take on an independent task and demonstrate their knowledge or creativity or practice a new skill. This is done in the immediate company of other learners and with an instructor nearby for reinforcement or assistance. The approach also showcases student work in real time in front of an audience of peers and encourages learners to do their best work.

- Engages each and every learner concurrently
- Enables real-time assessment of learner confidence and comprehension of the material at hand
- Provides a safe and motivating environment for learners to independently express themselves or apply new knowledge
- Allows the instructor to look over the shoulders of multiple learners at once and gauge understanding in real time

Suitable Venues

- Text chat room with multi-user whiteboard
- Virtual classroom
- Virtual meeting room or virtual office

Tools Used

- Multi-user whiteboard (which allows participants to navigate to their own screens or workspaces, sometimes called a "roam" feature)
- Text messaging or audio

Example Activity

Each math student in a live online activity is assigned a quadrant of a given whiteboard screen and then navigates to that screen on his or her own. Students are then all asked to draw the graph that would be expected from plotting a given mathematical equation (Figure 6.2). While the students are working, the instruc-

Figure 6.2. Solo Fishbowl.

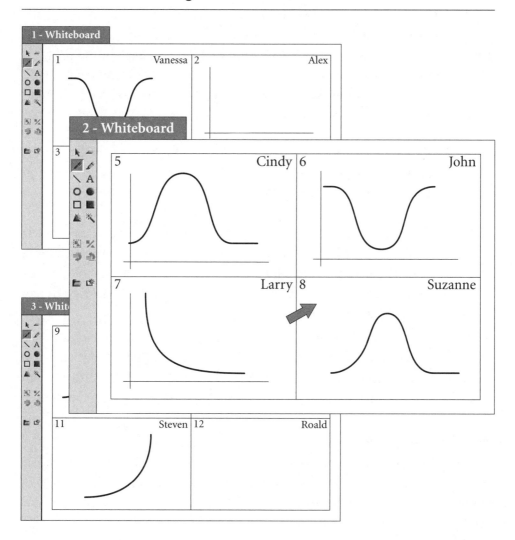

tor peruses the student work in progress and identifies examples worthy of sharing with the entire class. The facilitator then ends the exercise, brings everyone to one particular screen, highlights one of the learner responses, and asks the corresponding student to elaborate on her work. The instructor offers feedback or asks other students to comment. Other contributions are then showcased as appropriate.

Facilitation Tips

As you peruse each workspace or "fishbowl" during the exercise, refine or clarify the original instructions based on how work is proceeding. If work is not progressing as desired, consider pausing the activity prematurely and bringing the group back to the same screen for a mini-lesson or further guidance, or ask one student who is on the right track to explain to peers his or her thought process.

Other Applications

The Solo Fishbowl concept can be a useful technique for facilitating meetings or for peers conducting team projects. Additional applications may include

- Use the boxes for text submissions rather than drawings. Even if text chat messaging is available in the synchronous venue, the quadrants provide a more organized way to view, share, and highlight student work. For example, in a literature course, the boxes might be used to supply story themes, character descriptions, or literary devices.

- In any scenario-based learning situation, the boxes can be used to indicate what choices each learner would make at pivotal moments of a case study being read aloud by the instructor. The instructor would pause at each juncture and ask learners to note their decision in their box before proceeding with the story.

Variations on This Activity

One of a Kind. Ask learners to try to offer a response different from what is being suggested by peers sharing the same workspace. This will ensure a wider variety of responses and force learners not to go with the most obvious answer or the one that first comes to their mind.

Clockwise Critique. Ask everyone to move clockwise one box on their own screen and to use a different color whiteboard tool to annotate, grade, or comment upon the response offered by his or her peer. When learners are all brought back to the same screen, ask the peer reviewer rather than the original author to comment upon selected work. You might also use the Clockwise Critique as a way of obviating the need for full-group debriefing and therefore save time for other activities.

Within a Broader Online Learning Context

Responses shared in the fishbowl areas can be saved and posted into an online course area where they become the basis for asynchronous discussion or continued independent or group work. Responses might also be archived and then brought up again in a later live session or during an asynchronous activity.

PAIRED PARTNERS OR DYADS

Learners form pairs to collaborate in completing a real-time task. They may then share the results of their exchange with the full group for reflection, comparison, or debriefing.

Purpose

Paired Partner or dyad activities provide learners with an efficient way to work through material and safely share and test ideas with just one other person. When collaborating in pairs, it is difficult for any one learner to hide behind the anonymity of a larger group. Dyads can also be treated as teams to foster game-based learning situations, which energize and engage learners in healthy competition with other pairs, keeping everyone on task.

- Offers a more intimate and personalized approach to collaboration within a large group setting, and provides a safe format for dealing with sensitive issues that may be more difficult to broach in groups with many participants

- Taps into a coaching or mentoring dynamic when learners of varying abilities or skill levels are paired

- Acts as a bridge or transition into larger-scale collaborative activities (Palloff and Pratt, 2005)

Suitable Venues
- Instant messenger
- Text chat room
- Virtual classroom
- Virtual meeting room or virtual office
- MUVE

Tools Used

- Private text messaging
- Public text messaging
- Poll function useful but not required
- Audio communication optional

Example Activity

Learners are matched up with a peer who holds an opposing viewpoint on a controversial issue; they are then asked to present arguments to each other that support the *other* person's perspective. This forces the learners to think outside their comfort zone and to attempt to identify with someone by approaching a topic from a very different standpoint.

This sample activity comes from a class on biomedical ethics. The instructor briefly describes a patient's case in which euthanasia or physician-assisted suicide is being considered as an option for a terminally ill patient. After laying out the facts of the situation, the instructor uses a poll to gauge where learners stand on the issue, and facilitates the pairing of students with opposing opinions. Partners use the private messaging function to begin a text-based conversation with each other in which they use the first person to advance arguments supporting the opposing viewpoint. The facilitator then conducts a debriefing activity and asks learners to reflect on whether the exercise has softened, strengthened, or otherwise affected their own positions.

Facilitation Tips

Some chat venues allow the facilitator to observe private messages going back and forth between learners. If you are using such a platform, you may choose to observe and assess learner dialogues in action. Another suggestion is to ask students to copy and paste what they deem was their partner's strongest argument and paste that into the public chat area to kick start the debriefing aspect of the activity.

Other Applications

Paired Partner activities have wide-ranging potential within the live online environment to create a great deal of concurrent activity and to get learners thinking analytically and critically as they work with or question a peer. For instance:

- Foreign language skills
- Community-building exercises in which paired learners interview each other and then introduce their partners or their partners' ideas during a full group debriefing
- Role plays whereby pairs must stay in character as they discuss a given issue
- Consensus exercises

Variations on This Activity

Scoreboard. As pairs collaborate to address a series of questions via text messaging, they are asked to post their consensus responses on a public whiteboard screen. When all dyads' answers are on the board, or when the time allocated for the activity has run out, the facilitator goes through each team's responses and asks the group to score or rate each of them according to specified criteria.

Scavenger Hunt. Pairs may be asked to use their Web browser in conjunction with their private messaging channel to jointly research, locate, and discuss Web sites that respond to questions posed by the instructor.

Within a Broader Online Learning Context

Pairs that are formed during a synchronous session might be asked to continue working together on a follow-up assignment that stems from the real-time exercise. Pairs can be called upon to share the results of their ongoing collaboration in a subsequent live session. Each dyad might also be asked to copy and paste their private chat exchanges into a discussion board area on an online course Web site and conduct some asynchronous organization, analysis, and further research.

CRACKER BARRELS

During a live online Cracker Barrel activity, participants visit several virtual rooms in succession, where they find someone prepared to facilitate a conversation on a particular topic. After a given interval, everyone except the room's facilitator moves to another virtual space, where they take part in another brief discussion on a different topic led by another person (Figure 6.3). Live online Cracker Barrels are lively, fun, and relatively fast-paced. The concept of Cracker Barrel harkens back to the practice of community members gathering around a cracker-barrel in a country store for casual banter and conversation.

Figure 6.3. Cracker Barrels.

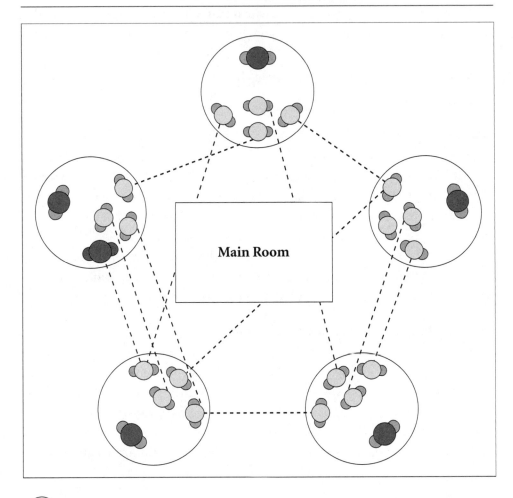

Breakout Room

Student Facilitator

Student Participants

Instructor

Student participants and instructor
move to new room every 15 minutes

Purpose

Online Cracker Barrels, especially when student-led, offer an opportunity for several learners to practice facilitating or leading presentations on topics they have researched or studied, while allowing their peers to absorb a great deal of information in an interactive manner in a short time. Student leaders improve with successive practice, learning from the questions and ideas generated in each session and incorporating what they learn into the remaining discussions.

Cracker Barrels are a fun, high-energy way to bring life to student projects that have been posted in an online course Web site. Moving from room to room during a Cracker Barrel is like changing the channel while watching television, thus mimicking an activity to which many learners today can relate.

- Fosters a supportive environment for students who learn by leading their peers through material they prepared

- Provides opportunity for several students to practice their delivery and communication skills in a concurrent learner-led format

- Builds student confidence through iterative practice and rehearsal in the company of peers

- Sets up an engaging and informal mechanism for students to showcase what they have learned and get feedback from others

- Offers an element of choice whereby participants are empowered to select their own path during the activity

- Affords opportunity to experience presenting a project before a live audience and extemporaneously responding to questions and critiques

Suitable Venues

- Virtual classroom
- Virtual meeting room or virtual office
- Instant messenger
- Text chat room
- MUVE
- Interactive Webcast

Tools Used

- Concurrently available channels or chat rooms, breakout rooms, or other discrete virtual spaces (including MUVE spaces)

- Public text messaging

- Slide showing, application sharing, Web browsing, or other visual display tools recommended

- Audio communication recommended

Example Activity

Prior to the live class session, an instructor in a course on advertising assigns each student to work independently to prepare a Web, radio, and television marketing campaign for one of three products: shampoo, orange juice, or tissues. The course structure already includes weekly ninety-minute live online class sessions, and the instructor plans a Cracker Barrel format for each of the next three sessions. During the Cracker Barrels, students make fifteen minute pitches to a room of their peers, showcasing their advertising strategy for their assigned products. In the intervening weeks between or before sessions, students study the collateral prepared by each presenter and post comments, analysis, and critiques in discussion boards.

Facilitation Tips

As the instructor, move throughout all of the rooms so that you can assess each learner's performance. Since some rooms will be unsupervised by an instructor during the activity (unless you have several teaching assistants on hand), you will want to remind everyone about respecting the facilitator in each room.

Other Applications

Cracker Barrels are suitable for learner-led exercises and for situations in which a number of guest experts are on hand concurrently, willing and ready to interact with learners based on learner interest.

- Virtual gallery talks and artistic critique sessions

- Show-and-tell exercises

- Presentations about any kind of student projects

- Book club, shared reading, or study group sessions, in which each room is led by someone who has read a segment of the class reading and is prepared to highlight and foster discussion on its major points

- Live online e-portfolio review sessions in which student papers, essays, or other projects form the basis for discussion within each room

- Student-led mini-lessons on assigned areas of the course or based on independent research

Variations on This Activity

Agora. The *agora* in ancient Greece was a marketplace in which people congregated to sell their wares and services, debate issues, and gather socially. In the Agora form of a Cracker Barrel, each learner makes his case or sells an idea. It can be a great activity format for persuasive speeches, debates, question-and-answer sessions, mock advertising pitches, or storytelling. Learners move from room to room, listen to and interact with each speaker, and then consider whose ideas they "buy."

Twenty Questions. The person leading each Cracker Barrel room can take on the role of a person, object, or concept, and visitors joining their Cracker Barrel sessions take turns asking questions to determine who or what the leader is playing. A competitive aspect might be added, whereby groups move as teams from room to room and accrue points for each rotation in which they correctly identify the role being played by the student leader.

Online PMQs. Online PMQs is an activity that encourages learners to be prepared to handle a heated barrage of questions. It is named for Prime Minister's Question Time, which is an opportunity for members of the British Parliament to ask the prime minister questions about government policies and current issues. Anyone who has ever seen a PMQ knows how fast-paced it can be, and how well prepared both those asking questions and the prime minister need to be. During PMQ Cracker Barrels, learners make a brief presentation to a group of peers who are expected to be prepared to ask hard-hitting questions. After ten or fifteen minutes, everyone rotates and a new set of learners takes on the prime minister role and responds to another torrent of peer questions. This method can be used in virtually any discipline.

Within a Broader Online Learning Context

The example activity already described illustrates how a Cracker Barrel can unfold over a series of live class meetings and make use of asynchronous discussion and evaluation tools to enhance the experience. Cracker Barrels can also be used in conjunction with large Webcasts as a way of adding more interactivity than would otherwise be possible in a large-broadcast setting. After a guest expert addresses a live group, learners can convene in theme-based Cracker Barrel sessions in which they reflect on what they just heard.

GUEST APPEARANCES AND CO-HOSTS

A live online learning event features an interactive guest appearance by a subject matter expert, professional located in the field, or another relevant authority. Alternatively, a guest or two joins the instructor to cofacilitate or co-host a live online session, offering a different perspective or taking part in an interview or panel-based conversation.

Purpose

Guest Appearances and Co-hosts provides an opportunity to vary the voice and perspective heard within a facilitated learning environment. Furthermore, it enhances the authenticity of the learning experience by incorporating access to a primary source with real-world experience. In the synchronous environment, guests are not bound by geographic location and can take part from literally anywhere in the world.

- Provides authentic learning experiences with access to primary sources
- Allows learners to interact with experts they might not otherwise meet
- Models discipline-specific conversations among professional colleagues
- Expands learner exposure to diverse perspectives and approaches to the field of study
- Opens up additional opportunities to engage and motivate learners by varying the format of learning activities in a course
- Encourages learners to seek out and connect with mentors, role models, and other human resources in the field

Suitable Venues

- Interactive Webcast
- Virtual classroom
- Virtual meeting room or virtual office
- Text chat room
- In-classroom aid

Tools Used

- Audio communication recommended
- Public text messaging, moderated if for a very large group
- Slide showing, application sharing, Web browsing, or other visual display tools recommended
- Live video if feasible

Example Activity

A professor of paleontology in North America invites a well-regarded paleontologist from Australia to interact with students in his online course during one of his upcoming evening office-hour sessions, which corresponds to the beginning of the work day in Australia. The Australian paleontologist e-mails her most recent articles and some digital images from a dinosaur dig to the professor so that he can post them in his online course site for students to review.

During the live session, the paleontologist talks about her work at the dig and shows and annotates images. Learners ask many questions, and in a characteristically spontaneous moment, the paleontologist turns on her Web camera to show some fossils sitting on the table next to her, and pans the lab, giving learners an inside look at an authentic dinosaur lab.

Facilitation Tips

It is often easier to get busy professionals to agree to a live online appearance, which has a specific start and end time, than it is to get a commitment for asynchronous participation. It can be hard for someone to estimate the time needed to be appropriately attentive to a discussion board forum over a period of several days or weeks. Guest appearances can also work well as an in-classroom aid during a face-to-face class. These multiple venue productions allow experts from anywhere around the globe to drop in and co-teach a lesson or make the subject matter immediately relevant to the world beyond the classroom.

Other Applications

Most learners love field trips, and guest appearances are like field trips that come right to them. An extra expert's voice can add credibility to a topic, and co-hosting provides instant interactivity, as learners enjoy the repartee between two professionals in the field.

- In nearly any discipline, experts can offer live critiques of student work, such as poetry, literature, photographs, or art.
- A real-life case study might unfold before students' eyes as the actual players in a scenario are brought into the virtual classroom, such as a lawyer and client modeling a deposition.
- First-hand accounts or anecdotes can be a very moving and powerful way to convey to learners the human impact of a given situation.
- Live dispatches from a field site or "on location" from a place of interest.
- In journalism or research courses, guests provide an opportunity to rehearse interviewing skills.
- Taking of oral or medical histories.

Variations on This Activity

Day in the Life. Turn on Web touring, pass the mouse to the guest expert, and ask him to show participants what Web sites he visits to stay current in his field.

Within a Broader Online Learning Context

As the paleontology example above suggests, one can use a guest appearance to anchor an otherwise asynchronous course with a live, special guest appearance by an outside expert. These sessions can provide an inspiring introduction to a topic or overall course, or a memorable capstone to tie things together. Special live guests can also be brought in to help resolve confusion, conflicts, and controversies within asynchronous discussion boards. Sometimes a new external voice in a different communication format can help break a deadlock or put things in context. Also, keep in mind that recordings or transcripts of guest appearances can usually be reused as asynchronous learning objects in a future offering of a course, whether or not the expert is again available to participate live online.

LIVE BLOGGING AND CCLOGGING

Learners independently type in reflections, learning moments, epiphanies, important facts, or concepts online in real time as a synchronous session unfolds. The result is a collection of informal student journals, also known as Web logs or *blogs*, which capture highlights of the event from each learner's perspective. Live blogging produces an on-demand and personalized record of a learning event for later review by each individual learner. The live blog can serve a similar function as traditional pen-based note taking, but with added benefits of accessibility, the potential to be archived and posted online, and direct links or synchronization with the material being covered.

In addition, live blogs can be integrated in a more public manner into a live event itself through a practice I call *cclogging,* or "closed captioning blogging," whereby rapid, real-time live blog commentary appears in a special live communication channel for others to view as a synchronous event or activity takes place. This practice is aided by the fact that a number of synchronous venues now offer a closed captioning (CC) channel with a primary goal of assisting those with disabilities or providing an avenue for real-time language translation. In addition to their invaluable assistive-technology role, these extra channels offer some added instructional opportunities, such as the posting of cclog commentaries by learners in real time during a live class activity.

Purpose

Live blogging and cclogging provide an informal, reflective, and kinetic outlet for learners and offer insight into what learners are thinking at any given moment during an instructional activity. Employing these techniques in a multichannel environment can open up a window into each learner's mind, offering the opportunity to provide immediate or just-in-time feedback or to improve current or future instruction. If the notion of "formative assessment" involves the ongoing review of teaching and learning over a full course of instruction, then perhaps live cclogging is formative assessment at its most extreme.

- Encourages learners to remain in an analytical, critical, or reflective mindset throughout a learning experience and keeps their minds active and engaged

- Provides an outlet and empowerment for more candid—and often more useful—responses and feedback through stream of consciousness communication

- Solicits feedback at the exact point of epiphany or frustration

- Keeps public channels clean and ready for open discussion

- Strengthens learner focus by providing a constant hands-on task

- Makes any necessary lecture segments more interactive and interesting

- Gives active learning opportunities during live broadcasts or interactive Webcasts

- Improves retention of material through active note taking

- Personalizes the record of the live experience for each individual learner

- Offers a unique journal-based assessment option by which an instructor can better understand learner mindsets

Suitable Venues

- Interactive Webcast

- Webcast

- Virtual classroom

- Virtual meeting room or virtual office

- Text chat room

- Instant messenger

- MUVE

Tools Used

- Private or public text messaging or

- Individual online note-taking tool or

- Integrated closed captioning or

- External discussion board or blog area or

- External instant messenger application

- Audio recommended as primary communications channel
(Live blogging via text works best when an overlying audio feed is the primary communications channel during the activity. It is usually too much to expect participants to participate in a text chat and engage in live blogging as well.)

Example Activity

In this example activity an instructor in a course on education looks for a meaningful way to provide a unifying look at how major learning theories relate to one another in real-world practice. She asks a handful of students in her audio- and text-based live virtual classroom session to assume the roles of different educational or psychological theorists. To facilitate the "casting" she displays a slide featuring a list of well-known contributors to the field of education, and uses the whiteboard to indicate which student has volunteered for which persona.

Once all the roles are assigned, the instructor assigns each "theorist" a closed captioning channel and titles these channels according to the theorist who will be operating them, such as Piaget, Gardner, Knowles, or Bruner. (If closed captioning channels were not available, an asynchronous discussion forum or blog within an online course could be substituted, or the public chat area could be used.)

The faculty leader then introduces the full class to an instructional design scenario—a situation in which a course or program needs to be created to meet a real-world learning need. The full class is charged with discussing the case to decide on an appropriate course of action for designing a course. The cast of theorists is asked to cclog or live blog the group discussion as though they were actually their assigned theorist. They are not directly part of the class conversation, but essentially float above it, looking down at it from a bird's eye perspective and saying what they would be thinking if they were quietly observing the class discussion unfold. Learners become keenly aware of how each learning theory is brought to bear in real-world scenarios and see the connection between theory and practice. Table 6.1 offers an extracted segment of this sample exercise as an illustration of the tone and pacing. The first column of the table depicts the time to provide a sense of the pacing of the activity. The second offers a transcription of what the instructor was saying into her microphone at that time. The last two columns show the text that two of the cclogging students were entering into their closed captioning channels.

Table 6.1. Live Blogging or Cclogging Example.

Time 🕐	Instructor 🔊 Voice—Live Audio	Student A: Bruner 📋 Text—Live Blog	Student B: Knowles 📋 Text—Live Blog
1:03	" . . . and most of the people in this training program will be between ages 55 and 65 and have been either employees or volunteers with the organization for an average of eight years . . ."	experience—they will have much to offer peers . during the training. probably want to avoid any kind of lecturing. As volunteers, they may be motivated enough for a constructivist approach to work . .	ahh, adult learners. sounds like we need to keep what we know about andragogy in mind, if you ask me . . .
1:06	" . . . so there is a lot of history, civics principles, and background that could be integrated for context. Ultimately they need to be able to operate the new machines."	Maybe we should ask them what they think is the best approach?	They are going to want to know why the new machines are being implemented. We can't just show up and start to show 'em how to use the equipment.
1:08	" . . . and the new machines have already been shipped—eight weeks before they are needed—so the training could happen right on site."	There's nothing like hands-on learning. Hmmm . . . how about weekly lessons where they solve a new problem each week and then you build on their success the following week?	Maybe you can simulate a real-world situation and have them play around with the machines. If they make a mistake, no biggie; they'll learn.

Facilitation Tips

- One of the cardinal rules of live blogging is that spelling and grammar are secondary to content. Encourage the use of short phrases, abbreviations, ellipses, comma-delineated phrases, or bullet points.

- Keep in mind the ringmaster guidelines for effective facilitation set forth in Chapter Five; in multichannel activities it is very useful to provide guidance to learners to help them focus on the right place at the right time.

- Depending on the maturity of your learners, you might also find it beneficial to set some ground rules for live blogging.

- Be clear about whether live blogging commentary will affect students' grades. To encourage the most candid, constructive blogging, it is often beneficial to inform learners that blogging will not adversely affect grades, but that good blogging will be noticed and rewarded.

Other Applications

Live blogging can be used in a multitude of settings. It can be particularly useful in situations where there are a large number of learners present and fewer opportunities for individualized interaction than might be desired. Live blogging of the event not only helps keep learners focused, but learners can go back later and read peers' blogs of the same event.

- In courses that deal with current events or communications, learners can meet in a chat room or virtual meeting room to live blog a particular speech, news event, or television program, offering their reflections commingled with others who may watching at the same time.

- In music courses, public live blogging may be employed to collect impressions of musical pieces as they are played in real time for a class assembled online.

Variations on This Activity

Pop-Up Video. Some live online courses integrate prerecorded media files such as video clips or animations. In a Pop-Up Video activity, participants are asked to offer their own captioning in public messaging areas as a video segment plays. Depending on the context, their subtitles might include questions the video raises for them, for instance.

Within a Broader Online Learning Context

Whether live blogs are used in the context of the live session or saved for review later, the running transcripts of each blogger's commentary can be copied and pasted into an online course site. Some instructors may incorporate live blog transcripts into the course e-portfolio; others may invite learners to post them to course discussion forums or asynchronous student blog areas, where they can be reviewed or annotated by the author, instructor, or others.

EXPEDITIONS AND VIRTUAL TRAINING LABS

The synchronous venue becomes a home base for guided but independent exploration. Learners congregate in real time for instruction and then are turned loose on the Web, referred to their own desktop applications, or directed to a virtual exhibit, lab, or primary resource to find an answer to a question, rehearse a skill, solve a problem, or complete a task. Upon returning to the home base, select learners share what they have found and how they located it, using text, voice, video, Web touring, application sharing, or other tools at their disposal.

Purpose

Expeditionary activities are a highly hands-on, constructivist form of instruction and assessment. They also connect learners to the vast array of resources available online and take advantage of the uniqueness of a classroom that is contiguous with the Web itself. Furthermore, with tools like application sharing and group Web browsing, students can easily take the reins and visually demonstrate their thought processes and practice new skills.

- Combine self-directed learning with the comfort and security of group and facilitated activities
- Provide an outlet for learners to behave in the manner they are accustomed to behaving when on the Web—clicking around and finding information independently—while still having live support on hand for guidance and validation
- Allow learners to practice using desktop and Web-based applications in a manner comparable to face-to-face computer lab settings where an instructor can look over their shoulders

Suitable Venues

- Virtual classroom
- Virtual meeting room or virtual office
- Adaptable to virtual reference desk for tutoring purposes

Tools Used

- Independent Web browsing and group Web touring
- Application sharing led by instructor and participants
- Two-way audio recommended
- Text messaging useful

Example Activity

The instructor of a research methods and statistics course offers a series of live online and "hands-on" virtual lab sessions designed to train her students on the use of the statistics software that they will be using in their class. The lab sessions are offered in three identical "sections" so that students may choose the one that best fits their schedule and to keep each workshop at a size that allows highly individualized coaching.

During the live lab, participants open up their statistics software and follow along as the instructor uses application sharing to introduce a few important features. She gives participants instructions to complete certain tasks on their own, and periodically enables remote desktop sharing so that she can "look over the shoulder" of some of her learners and see how they are progressing. From time to time, she calls upon a student, allows him to broadcast his application to the group, and asks him to demonstrate a particular aspect of the program.

Combining software training on the statistics program with the research methods component of her course, she then sends learners out to the Web to locate reliable datasets containing sea-level readings in certain coastal areas. As students "return" with the data, some are called upon to show their desktops, explain how they found and verified the information, and then walk their peers through the process of importing the data into the statistics program.

Facilitation Tips

Resist the urge to do all of the driving of the mouse. When it comes to learning how to use software or navigate a Web site, most people will retain more from actively clicking around the application than from more passively listening or watching someone else walk through the steps. Even when you want to demonstrate something, consider passing mouse control to a learner instead. If they know what to do you can let them proceed to show the rest of the class. If they need guidance, you can vocally walk them through the steps while they actually do the navigating and clicking. The other learners in the class often pay closer attention when their peers are "driving" the mouse than when their instructor is leading, if for no other reason than it sets the stage that *they* may be next to take control and they need to be ready and focused.

Other Applications

- Use existing multimedia components to provide facilitated lab-like experiences. Many learning object repositories contain links to modules such as virtual dissections, gravity simulators, or dynamic supply and demand charts.

- Expeditionary Web browsing can also be used to visit primary resources on the Web and to teach learners about everything from information literacy to Internet safety.

Variations on This Activity

Virtual Reference Desk. The techniques described for expeditions and virtual labs work very well in one-on-one situations as well. Whether you are providing the just-in-time guidance a learner needs to find the right library databases or meeting a student online to review suggested edits to a paper, a virtual reference desk approach can help keep students stay on track.

Within a Broader Online Learning Context

Expeditions do not need to go very far from home to be valuable to students. Take students on a field trip to the Web site for their own course, provide a tour of the coming week's assignments and materials, or showcase student work posted on the site. End a live online session with an expedition to a pristine discussion board area set up for the coming week, and ask learners to take the last three minutes of the live class to make their first asynchronous post of the week. This seamlessly connects the synchronous class to the other aspects of the course, and keeps momentum generated during the live event going even after you log off.

MULTIPLE VENUE PRODUCTIONS OR PRESENTATIONS

Multiple venue productions or presentations (MVPs) are live online learning activities that connect those participating *online* as individuals with one or more groups of people assembled together in *face-to-face* settings.

The concept of hybrid forms of live technology-mediated learning is not new, as institutions have been combining things such as satellite and videoconferencing delivery with physical classroom venues for some time. However, the combination of multichanneled online tools, ever-improving Internet-based audio and video, highly accessible high-bandwidth connectivity, and mobile computing devices does provide educators with what Dan Balzer calls new and "intriguing permutation[s]" of what has been possible to date (2005).

The vast number of permutations for combining synchronous tools and venues with physical ones puts someone crafting an MVP experience into the shoes of a musical composer and conductor. Each venue involved is like another instrument that needs to be addressed in the score and guided during the performance. And while individual groups need to be coordinated and prepared in advance to do their part, the producer of an MVP needs to keep the big picture in mind as well: what is the overall impact and is it worth it? As with designing any instructional experience, the effort required to produce an effective MVP should always be measured against the potential return on that investment of time and energy.

Purpose

The MVP genre of synchronous learning events can serve many ends but most strive to produce an experience in which every participant feels connected, involved, and integral to the experience. Everyone knows why they are present. An MVP

- Enables many individuals and sites to participate in a unique or one-time event as it takes place live
- Provides opportunities to bridge an interactive face-to-face learning activity out to students not able to be present at the originating location
- Offers various groups concurrent access to a common live source of information or knowledge, while allowing them to easily retreat to the company of their local colleagues for reflection and action specific to their situation

- Through its scale and one-of-a-kind nature, creates a sense of momentousness among participants that can lead to increased engagement, excitement, and retention of knowledge

Suitable Venues
- Virtually any appropriate mix of synchronous venues and Web-connected physical gathering spaces

Tools Used
- Multiway audio and video recommended
- Slide and media-showing functions
- Whiteboard and application sharing
- Public and private text messaging
- In-room: appropriate speakers, microphones, or house audio or public address system; connectivity (wireless a plus); multiple computer stations or kiosks to reduce person-to-computer ratio; suitably sized projection screen

Figure 6.4 illustrates some of the many ways in which learners, facilitators, presenters, groups, and individuals can take part in an MVP. Note that a facilitator is often just one coordinating party involved; on-site technicians, panelists, and presenters at various venues often play significant roles as well.

Example Activity
A renowned psychologist is paying a rare visit to conduct a workshop on a university campus. Because of the significance of the visitor and his work, the university extends an invitation for outside students, experts, and instructors to take part in the event either by joining the session on campus or participating online. Due to the dynamic nature of the content and the speaker, the workshop organizers want more than simply to provide remote participants with a one-way audio or video feed; they want to allow all audience members to participate freely with the expert and with one another. The visiting psychologist accedes and is excited to be part of a unique event of this kind; he even invites some colleagues from his home country to login and participate live as co-panelists.

Figure 6.4. Example of Multiple Venue Presentation Configuration.

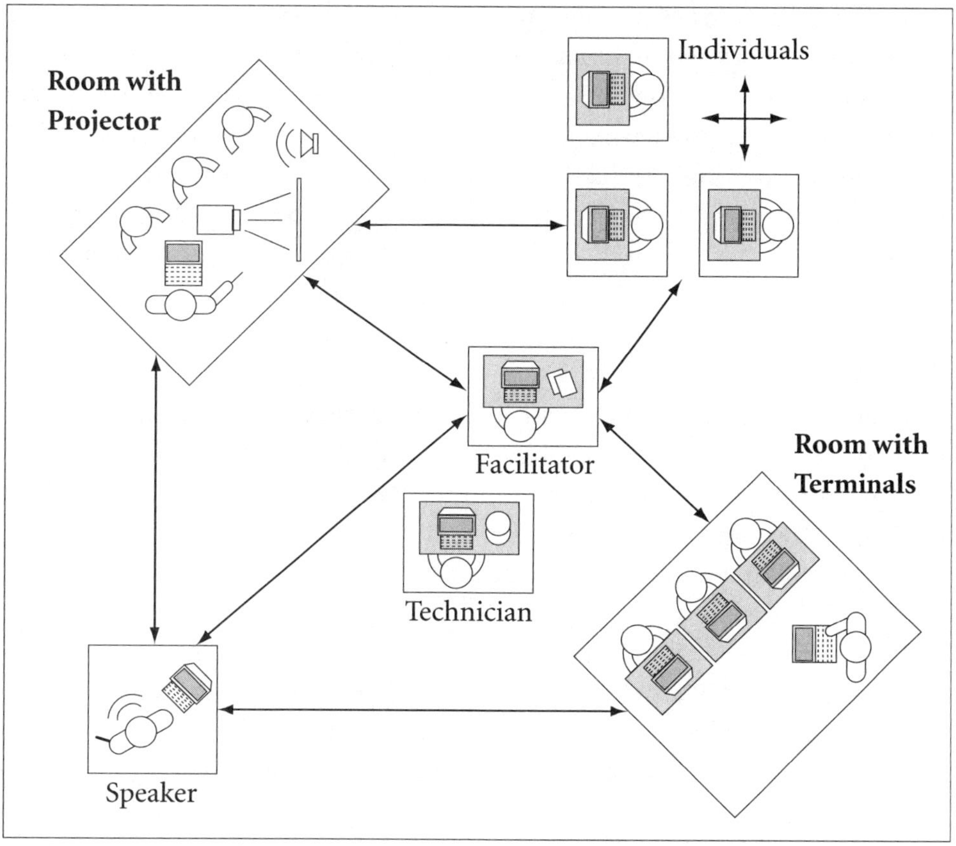

Source: Illustration by Randall Kindley.

During the live event, the psychologist is seated at a table with a faculty member who is serving as the Web moderator, providing a bridge between online participants and those in the physical room with the psychologist. A projection screen displays a virtual classroom interface, which will be carrying an audio and video feed from the room out to the Web. At a few remote campuses, instructors have invited their students to join them in a Web-connected classroom to take part as a group. Those with laptops bring them to class to connect individually, while the rest watch a projected virtual classroom interface controlled by the instructor at the front of the room. Other individuals who are not campus-based login on their own from their homes or offices.

The event proceeds with some introductory remarks from the expert and some additional comments from the speaker's colleagues connected remotely, and then moves to a discussion period. At one point, the facilitator suggests that participants at each venue take about ten or fifteen minutes to discuss a series of issues on their own, perhaps applying them to their own class contexts. Those connected as individuals online retire to a breakout room to meet each other. All venues are then invited back, at which point the facilitator asks for one or two groups to share any questions that have emerged from their clustered conversations.

Facilitation Tips

One common mistake when facilitating MVPs is to neglect one participating venue at the expense of another, causing loss of goodwill. Because every physical site can have its own unique considerations, audience composition, and reason for participating, it is very important to understand these variables as well as possible. During an MVP session, a facilitator should check in with each venue and make sure they feel connected.

Because of the potential volume of feedback and questions from various venues during a live MVP, a Web moderator can review questions and comments, consolidate themes, and then share specific responses with the key panelists. Polls and whiteboard grids with a box for each venue can also be useful tools for organizing MVP activity.

If appropriate to the context, one might want to generate handouts for advance distribution to the various venues. These packets might include suggested discussion topics for moments during the MVP when facilitators at each physical venue are asked to lead activities specific to their own sites.

Where feasible, MVPs can benefit from the availability of multiple computers at a given face-to-face location. The more people who can physically have their fingers on a keyboard and mouse or be in front of a microphone, the more connected and engaged people will feel to the overall experience.

Variations on This Activity

The connection of people on wireless devices—located anywhere in the world—certainly offers one intriguing twist to the notion of what constitutes a *venue*.

Additional Resources

FURTHER READING AND RELATED WEB SITES

Book Companion

The following Web site is maintained by the author of this book and offers access to synchronous venues, resources, and current links related to learning in real time:

http://www.LearningInRealTime.com

Online Communities

These sites are online communities of education and training professionals who use synchronous tools in their instruction. Free live events are offered regularly.

http://www.learningtimes.org
http://home.learningtimes.net/lta
http://home.learningtimes.net/cstp

Synchronous Certification

The following site offers a formal certification program for educators and trainers who design and deliver synchronous instruction:

http://www.learningtimes.net/cert

Synchronous Activities

These books provide ideas for designing and managing synchronous activities:

Hofmann, J. *Live and Online: Tips, Techniques, and Ready-to-Use Activities for the Virtual Classroom.* San Francisco: Pfeiffer, 2004.

Hofmann, J. *The Synchronous Trainer's Survival Guide: Facilitating Successful Live and Online Courses, Meetings, and Events.* San Francisco: Pfeiffer, 2003.

Assessing Online Collaboration

The following resource offers suggestions for assessing collaborative online learning activities:

Palloff, M., and Pratt, K. *Collaborating Online: Learning Together in Community.* San Francisco: Jossey-Bass, 2005.

Asynchronous Learning Activities

Interaction and collaboration in synchronous venues often begins or continues in asynchronous forums as well. These resources provide ideas for asynchronous activities that engage learners:

http://www.thiagi.com

Conrad, R., and Donaldson, J. *Engaging the Online Learner: Activities and Resources for Creative Instruction.* San Francisco: Jossey-Bass, 2004.

Recognition of Achievement in Synchronous Instruction

Synchronous instruction is an evolving field. The following site recognizes innovation and achievement in designing online learning experiences and programs that are worthy of the live medium:

http://www.TheLolas.com

TEN COMMON MISCONCEPTIONS ABOUT SYNCHRONOUS INSTRUCTION

1. It defeats the whole reason that learners take courses online: any*time,* anywhere!
2. Instructors who deliver synchronous instruction don't believe in the value of asynchronous instruction.
3. Real-time learning means lots of quick typing.
4. Learning in real time does not offer adequate time to reflect before offering a response.
5. Synchronous online communication requires a lot of special equipment and takes up too much bandwidth.
6. Synchronous venues are all about bringing the lecture live online, and there is no need for that.
7. Full-screen video or bust.
8. Real-time online tools are expensive.
9. Synchronous interaction is too difficult to learn and is hard to facilitate.
10. The technology has not arrived or matured yet.

1. *It defeats the whole reason that learners take courses online: anytime, anywhere!* The reason learners take courses online is *to learn.* They place trust in instructors that they will craft the highest-quality, most efficient path for them to garner the skills or knowledge they are seeking. Some, although by no means all, of these skills are best learned in real time. Substituting another approach when real-time learning is most appropriate and available diminishes the educational potential of the experience. Synchronous learning *does* afford the convenience of "anywhere" learning—requiring no commute, no proper attire, and no physical overhead—and can even hold fast to the "anytime" mantra through the availability of recordings, multiple time offerings, impromptu, just-in-time communication, and collaboration with peers at mutually convenient times. When synchronous learning is deemed necessary, as long as you tell learners up front that real-time participation will be expected to ensure the quality of their learning experience, they can be trusted to decide whether to enroll or not.

2. *Instructors who deliver synchronous instruction don't believe in the value of asynchronous instruction.* People who deliver synchronous instruction usually *do* rely heavily upon and believe strongly in the value of asynchronous communications, without which many of their live interactions would lack an important and necessary context. Most synchronous experiences do not live in isolation; they build off asynchronous resources and lead back to asynchronous resources. For some reason, there are some who have artificially divided the world into *asynchronous* and *synchronous* "camps" and imply that learning must be one or the other. Learning happens over a very broad continuum—online, offline, from books, friends, mentors, accidents, amusement parks, chalkboards, nature, computers, you name it—and dividing the world so rigidly along this one plane runs the risk of missing some really unexpected and wonderful learning opportunities. The synchronous realm itself encompasses a diverse range of communication options—from the impromptu student question via instant messenger to self-organizing group meetings to hands-on workshops with a full class of learners—and lumping all of the real-time possibilities into one simple category in order to promptly dismiss them undermines the ultimate goal: designing the best learning experiences possible.

3. *Real-time learning means lots of quick typing.* While the earliest forms of synchronous interaction were completely text-based, the synchronous landscape has rapidly evolved to include robust options that integrate voice, video, shared visuals and media, and other interactive tools. Using real-time learning environments no longer must mean that the "fastest typist wins."

4. *Learning in real time does not offer adequate time to reflect before offering a response.* This is true, but to some extent, that is the point. Many aspects of life and work require us to communicate extemporaneously or solve problems with little notice and without the luxury of hours of contemplation. These are important skills to hone, and in the study of some fields, we wouldn't want our learners to leave our influence without the knowledge that they possessed these skills. When sufficient time for reflection is needed, asynchronous options should be considered over real-time venues. American essayist Agnes Repplier wrote in 1904: "It is not what we learn in conversation that enriches us. It is the elation that comes of swift contact with tingling currents of thought." Well-facilitated synchronous learning experiences can be vibrantly paced and can advance a conversation far more quickly, and take it to far more places in far less time, than a discussion that unfolds

in an asynchronous manner. We should remember that this is part of the charm and benefit of real-time interaction, not necessarily its weakness.

5. *Synchronous online communication requires a lot of special equipment and takes up too much bandwidth.* Although there are forms of technology-based, real-time communication for which this is true, there is an entire and rapidly expanding industry based on online tools that work on most existing home and office computers and laptops—and on handheld devices and mobile phones as well. They require nothing more than a basic Internet connection; many tools, even a great number that offer live audio interaction, work quite satisfactorily on dial-up connections. Hearing synchronous audio requires speakers or headphones, and the transmitting of one's voice requires a microphone, most of which come standard with newer computer packages or can be purchased quite inexpensively at a local computer shop. Some systems will substitute the phone for the aforementioned equipment, meaning that no sound peripherals are needed at all. Video communication adds the requirement of a Web camera or better equipment, depending on the quality desired, but even live video interaction is no longer relegated to the realm of bulky videoconferencing systems, special satellite studios, or mega-bandwidth operations.

6. *Synchronous venues are all about bringing the lecture live online, and there is no need for that.* Synchronous venues are at least as flexible in terms of the kind of learning they support as empty classrooms or lecture halls. Technology does not lecture; people do. And despite the fact that there may be many people who have brought their offline lecturing approaches to live online venues, often to ill effect, real-time online learning venues offer an entirely new form of human communication and learning opportunity. Those who value learning and are innovative in how they help students achieve learning objectives have a field day crafting methods to use live online environments in ways that are as far from the lecture as imaginable. Synchronous learning is at its best when it is being used to do live online that cannot be achieved in any other available manner. That rarely includes lecturing.

7. *Full-screen video or bust.* Understandably, some argue that until synchronous venues support full-screen, full-motion video, they will never be able to replicate the physical classroom experience. Notwithstanding the fact that more and more live online systems already support full-screen video—albeit with sufficient

bandwidth required, the availability of which is also increasing—the premise that big and beautiful live video is a prerequisite for live online learning or that the ultimate goal is to replicate the physical classroom is flawed. We don't necessarily want to duplicate the physical classroom; not all activity that happens in that "full motion video" environment we call the classroom is worthy of imitation. We ultimately want to use the opportunity afforded by these completely new online environments to improve how people learn. To some extent, reliance on true-to-life video provides a crutch that may cause some to miss a window of opportunity to re-invent their live instruction. For years now, instructors and students have been using a rich array of real-time online tools in some very powerful and innovative ways, often without video. It will be exciting to see how the addition of full-screen video builds on their creative approaches, rather than replaces them.

8. *Real-time online tools are expensive.* It is not difficult to see why this notion exists. In the early days of adoption of course management systems (CMS), synchronous platforms usually cost many times the price of the CMS, which was often free or nearly free, relative to the live system. Online course platforms have since grown to be a significant investment for most organizations, while synchronous tool prices have fallen. Furthermore, due to market pressure, pricing options that allow individual faculty members to add real-time components to their classes without involving institutional purchase processes are becoming more prevalent, including a number of pay-per-use or monthly subscription options. Notwithstanding these adjustments, virtual classrooms can still cost more than individual faculty budgets can afford. This is prompting department, institutional, and consortium purchases of synchronous tools for shared use. The proliferation of free instant messenger tools, most now with audio and video support, and the bundling of real-time communication tools into operating systems will continue to exert downward pricing pressure on more specialized synchronous learning tools. Fully functioning, open-source synchronous systems will also be on the horizon. All that aside, it is important to consider what real-time, personal interaction that makes learning online about as human as humanly possible is ultimately worth for a given educational context. Often, a properly considered investment is deemed well worthwhile.

9. *Synchronous interaction is too difficult to learn and is hard to facilitate.* Nothing is too difficult to learn, especially for people who make their careers out of educating others. The best way to learn how to *teach* with a synchronous tool is to

learn with one. There are a great number of free and fee-based resources to gain hands-on experience in using synchronous tools, and even to get certified in teaching with them. This book's Web site, www.LearningInRealTime.com, lists some of these resources. Tools range in complexity from simple instant messengers that truly anyone who can use a computer can master to more advanced virtual classrooms that can feel like a cockpit and require more practice. Facilitating is truly a skill that must be practiced to be perfected, and practice requires the presence of real people requiring facilitation. For that reason, those with a desire and a need to be engaged in the synchronous realm should seek out any human support they need, and then jump in and begin interacting or facilitating live online. The best-designed online learning venues available will ultimately allow you to focus more on students and colleagues than on the clicking of buttons required to interact with them.

10. *The technology has not arrived or matured yet.* No, it is here, it is eminently useable, and it keeps getting better. People who may have experienced a live virtual classroom many years ago, when the concept of live audio communication on the Web was new and the technologies still rather unreliable, are revisiting the synchronous arena to find a very different landscape and set of available resources. With millions worldwide using instant messengers and turning their computing devices into phones and conferencing tools to interact with others across the globe, live Web communication has fast become a commodity upon which many people rely for essential communications. Although the tools have not fully matured, few Web technologies have, since the pace of progress is so rapid and there is plenty of potential for continued innovation. There are ample tools available with track records for success in enabling real-time live online communication such that the user's focus can remain more on facilitating quality learning experiences than on crossing fingers and hoping things don't break. If you are waiting for it to become safe to engage in synchronous interaction online, that time has arrived.

SCHEDULING SYNCHRONOUS INTERACTION

One of the more common concerns when employing synchronous interaction within the online learning environment stems directly from the venue's live nature itself: scheduling. The following list sets forth some practical suggestions to help integrate live interaction into a context in which learners are concerned about flexibility and time zones are blurred by global participation.

- Manage expectations from the very beginning.
- Record real-time activities.
- Offer multiple live sections.
- Don't schedule: make use of impromptu venues for just-in-time collaboration and support.
- Form student groups for real-time activities.
- Use polls as scheduling aids.
- Use online time zone resources when selecting live meeting times.
- Make synchronous sessions optional.
- Invite pre- and post-event questions and comments.
- Partner with colleagues or institutions in different time zones.
- Employ real-time interaction when it's really right.

- *Manage expectations from the very beginning.* If a decision has been made to require synchronous participation in an online course, include these time expectations in the course catalog. Some institutions with online offerings will use icons in their course listings to easily denote classes or programs with required synchronous components. It is much harder to introduce and mandate synchronous interaction once a course is under way. Set expectations up front.

- *Record real-time activities.* Although they generally lack the ability to interact with live peers and facilitators, recordings are a reasonable substitute for someone who cannot attend a live class activity—or wishes to see it again, for that matter. Archived live sessions or transcripts often see far more traffic than the initial live events they captured. Also, consider asking a participant who attends a live session to post some notes, highlights, or minutes to an online course site for others to view. This can also be used to stimulate continued asynchronous dialogue.

• *Offer multiple live sections.* Offering more than one opportunity to meet in real time for a class activity gives learners more flexibility. Instead of one session, for example, one might offer two meeting times and vary the day of the week and the start time to accommodate recurring learner commitments and time preferences. Having more time options also usually means having smaller groups, which can translate to more individualized instruction time with learners. Multiple sessions can be led by co-facilitators, teaching assistants, or even students themselves.

• *Don't schedule: make use of impromptu venues for just-in-time collaboration and support.* Some of the most meaningful learning happens in informal venues, outside of scheduled class times, when learners interact with each other and with their instructor. Encourage learners to use instant messengers or virtual offices to communicate with you, with their peers, or with available live online library or support resources.

• *Form student groups for real-time activities.* Peer-to-peer interaction is more scaleable than instructor-to-peer interaction. If the subject matter and learning objectives will benefit from group collaboration and scheduling a single session is impractical, form student groups based on time zones or time preferences and ask peers to meet on their own. Encourage groups to record sessions, or post meeting summaries or responses to assignments conducted during their meetings in asynchronous forums to document their work and progress.

• *Use polls as scheduling aids.* There are a number of tools in online course platforms and freely available on the Web that enable one to easily conduct polls or surveys. As a facilitator trying to schedule synchronous sessions, create a Web-based poll based on a variety of times and days that work for you, and then open the poll to participants for a short window of time so that all may register their preferences. Quickly finalize live session times accordingly after the poll closes, as people are busy and their schedules tend to change rapidly. Consider making the poll results nonanonymous, so that if a session time is good for everyone except for one or two people, you know who to contact directly to discuss alternate arrangements.

• *Use online time zone resources when selecting live meeting times.* Enter the phrase "time zone" into your favorite search engine and find a set of resources that translate potential meeting times into other time zones and help pinpoint what constitutes waking hours concurrently in selected locales across the globe. Use these resources to aid in scheduling events. (You can also find links to some of these resources at this book's Web site at www.LearningInRealTime.com.)

- *Make synchronous sessions optional.* If scheduled real-time interaction would be a nice-to-have option but is not required for learning the material at hand, consider offering scheduled live sessions at which attendance is optional. Events might include office hours, review sessions, or appearances by guest experts. Motivated learners and those looking for greater access to the instructor or peers will find time to participate; others may choose to review recordings or transcripts.

- *Invite pre- and post-event questions and comments.* Invite learners who cannot attend scheduled live online activities to post questions or comments in advance to an asynchronous discussion forum. Respond to their contributions during the live event, even referencing the specific questions and learners' names to make them feel a part of the process when they view the recording or transcript. Be available to respond to follow-up questions that are posted asynchronously when a recording is viewed.

- *Partner with colleagues or institutions in different time zones.* A growing number of faculty and institutions are partnering with counterparts in other time zones or countries to increase their ability to provide live online support and instruction to a population of learners that knows no geographic or time-based boundaries.

- *Employ real-time interaction when it's really right.* Above all, only require synchronous interaction when it is the best way for learners to achieve stated learning objectives. When you are confident in that decision, scheduling options fall into place.

BUYER'S GUIDE: QUESTIONS TO ASK WHEN CONSIDERING A SYNCHRONOUS TOOL

Certainly the most important question to ask when considering the acquisition of a synchronous platform is the question you ask yourself: *Will the tool meet our learning needs?* You will of course want to make sure it has all of the specific features you are seeking, and perhaps a few more than you need to provide some flexibility down the road. The table that follows does not attempt to answer those very individualized questions. Instead it provides a list of things to ask the provider of the tool being considered, regardless of the instructional goal and desired features list, that may not always be so obvious to inquire about.

What to Ask	Why It Matters
Is the product cross-platform?	A venue that is cross-platform works properly on multiple computer operating systems, such as Windows, Macintosh, and Linux. In learning situations in which you have no control over and do not know what kind of computers your learners are using, choosing a real-time tool that has been tested and is designed to work on all of the major operating systems is very important. You also want to know whether there are certain features that do not work or that work substantially differently on some platforms versus others; this is not an uncommon phenomenon and you should know in advance whether any features you intend to use fit into this category.
Does it work on all Web browsers?	The Web browser is the application one uses to explore the World Wide Web. There are many Web browsers and versions of each in use by learners. You simply want to know which browsers and browser versions are tested to work with the given platform so that you can decide whether any undue burden will be placed on your learners or whether anyone will be excluded from participating.
Does the audio or video transmission have any latency?	Most tools that transmit audio or video on the Web will have some degree of latency—a delay between the time something is actually said or done and the time those words or images arrive for remote participants. The range can be from an almost imperceptible fraction of a second to upwards of half a minute. Traditionally, latency has been used to improve the quality of

(Continued)

| | transmission by offering a buffer on which to draw when Internet conditions are poor; however, there are now many innovative protocols that ensure quality while keeping latency very low. Look for systems with virtually no latency for your real-time learning applications; getting instant feedback from learners is crucial, and this is very difficult when communication times are artificially long. |

Are learners with disabilities afforded an acceptable real-time experience?

Real-time venues have incredible potential for creating a sense of community and fostering collaboration and group learning. Yet this promise cannot be realized if learners with disabilities are excluded from participating. Investigate how the tool you are considering adheres to standards and regulations and works with assistive technologies for accommodating the needs of those with disabilities.

Does it have a multi-user, object-oriented whiteboard?

Object-oriented means that objects—such as images, lines, or annotations—can be moved around the whiteboard once they are placed there, and *multi-user* means that more than one participant can add to or edit the contents of the whiteboard at the same time. Both of these features open a wide array of collaborative options for learning that make the system far more than a slide viewer.

What software, if any, needs to be downloaded and how big is the file?

Some venues require learners to download software upon entering. It is good to know how large such downloads are so that you can properly warn learners on slower speed connections how much time to allot in preparing to login the first time.

How many people can be in one virtual room at a time?

You are interested to know how many people can be safely connected to a single virtual room at one time and what kind of testing has been done to ensure that the system does not get unstable when, say, the fifteenth person logs in.

Where do recordings reside?

Some systems with a recording feature store those recordings centrally on a server, whereas others store them locally on each participant's computer. There are reasons you might like either scenario (for example, control over ownership of content or ability to control when a recording is no longer available). You do want to know whether your recordings can play back independently should you no longer have access to the synchronous tool that was used to create them.

Will it work through most firewalls?	Firewalls are used by organizations and individuals to protect their networks and computers from malicious outside activity. Since firewalls are extremely common—and they are not always immediately accepting of the kind of activity generated by synchronous participation—it is important to know how a venue "plays nice" with firewalls and allows learners to take part in a real-time activity with no or minimal adjustments.
What happens when upgrades are available?	You want to be aware of the process by which new versions of the synchronous venue become available to learners. It is very useful to know things such as whether upgrades happen automatically, how much advance notice is given to the instructor, and when training or documentation is made available.
Does it integrate with other Web sites and online course systems?	The use of synchronous venues rarely happens in isolation. You want to know what methods are available to integrate the real-time tool into your course, library, or other Web site or system so that learners can sail seamlessly from one resource to another.
What kind of human support is available?	When crises occur with synchronous tools, one often can't wait until tomorrow for assistance. Be aware of what kind of live and on-demand support resources are available should help be needed in real time.
How does the system deal with poor or low-speed connections?	Despite improving bandwidth, we are in a global learning environment where we do not necessarily know the quality of any learner's Internet connection at any given time. We want to know how a synchronous tool adjusts to poor or low-speed connections, and whether the resulting experience would be sufficient for a learner to still find the activity meaningful.
Can one try the tool in a real-world situation before making a decision?	Synchronous products are hands-on applications. See whether you can get your hands on a useable version of a product before you lock yourself into it and use it in a real-world situation with learners.
Are recordings editable?	Post-production of a recording can be very useful to edit out sections that are not relevant or not appropriate for on-demand viewers.
What technical configuration tests are available for learners?	Some providers offer Web-based tools that are accessed in advance of a live session to simulate the technical demands placed on a learner's computer by the product. They then

(Continued)

What to Ask	Why It Matters
	indicate whether the computer meets the conditions needed to participate in a live session and offer specific troubleshooting guidance when it does not. This helps reduce technical problems in actual live sessions and keeps the focus on the learning at hand.
What kind of security or encryption is available?	Depending on the nature of your live activities, you may be concerned about what kinds of safeguards are available to prevent savvy hackers or curiosity seekers from accessing the information being exchanged during live sessions. Different options can be available.
Is the tool hosted by the vendor or available to house on your own site?	Many providers offer the option to load the synchronous software onto your own computer network, or to access it in a service provider model off of their network. This is an important decision that involves many factors, but ultimately you want to be aware of any hidden costs and tasks associated with each option. Ask what those are up front.
How often are new versions released?	Knowing the provider's upgrade schedule not only helps you prepare for future changes in the tool, but also gives you a sense of the provider's track record in innovating and keeping up in a fast-paced world.
What is the process for determining what features appear in new versions?	It is informative to find out how responsive the provider is to the input of those using the product in the field and how your suggestions for improvements will be taken into account.
Who is the typical user?	Synchronous products can appeal to people in a range of fields and industries. Some work well across disciplines, whereas others are more specialized for a certain kind of user. Take time to learn who the provider considers their typical user. This is a good indicator as to whether your needs will be considered as the product develops. If the provider has a client educational advisory board, for example, this is a sign that the needs of educators are being duly considered.

References

Ambady, N., and Rosenthal, R. "Half a Minute: Predicting Teacher Evaluations from Thin Slices of Behavior and Physical Attractiveness." *Journal of Personality and Social Psychology,* 1993, *64,* 431.

"Assessment of 21st Century Skills: The Current Landscape." Washington: Partnership for 21st Century Skills, June 2005, http://www.21stcenturyskills.org/images/stories/otherdocs/Assessment_Landscape.pdf. Retrieved July 1, 2005.

Balzer, D. "Facilitating at the Crossroads: The Emergence of Multiple Venue Productions/Presentations (MVPs)." *ION Research Case Studies, 3*(2), http://www.ion.illinois.edu/resources/casestudies/vol3num2/dbalzer/index.asp. Retrieved May 20, 2005.

Baringer, D., and McCroskey, J. "Immediacy in the Classroom: Student Immediacy." *Communication Education,* April 2000, *49*(2), 178.

Bruce, R. *Bell: Alexander Graham Bell and the Conquest of Solitude.* Boston: Little, Brown, 1973.

Carter, K. "Type Me How You Feel: Quasi-Nonverbal Cues in Computer-Mediated Communication." *ETC: A Review of General Semantics,* Spring 2003, *60*(1), 29.

Chen, H., and Mazow, C. "Electronic Learning Portfolios and Student Affairs." *Stanford Center for Innovations in Learning,* October 28, 2002, http://www.naspa.org/netresults/PrinterFriendly.cfm?ID=825. Retrieved May 30, 2005.

Chickering, A., and Ehrmann, S. "Implementing the Seven Principles: Technology as Lever." *AAHE Bulletin.* Washington: American Association for Higher Education, March 1996.

Chickering, A., and Ehrmann, S. "Webcast Archive—The Seven Principles, Assessment, and Technology: A Little History." October 27, 2003, http://home.learningtimes.net/tltgroup?go=252312. Retrieved June 30, 2005.

Chickering, A., and Gamson, Z. "Seven Principles for Good Practice in Undergraduate Education." *AAHE Bulletin.* Washington: American Association for Higher Education, March 1987.

Coghlan, M. "How Important Are Synchronous Tools in Web-Based Teaching and Learning Environments?" May 2004a, http://users.chariot.net.au/~michaelc/synch/surv_discuss.htm. Retrieved April 30, 2005.

Coghlan, M. "Finding Your Voice Online: An Inquiry into the Use of Online Voice Applications in Higher Education." *The Knowledge Tree,* 5, June 2004b. http://www.elearn.wa.edu.au/kt/edition05/html/npra_michael_coghlan.html. Retrieved April 1, 2005.

Conderman, G., and McCarty, B. "Shared Insights from University Co-Teaching." *Academic Exchange Quarterly,* Winter 2003, *7*(4), http://www.rapidintellect.com/AEQweb/choice2z.htm. Retrieved June 15, 2005.

Conrad, R., and Donaldson, J. *Engaging the Online Learner: Activities and Resources for Creative Instruction.* San Francisco: Jossey-Bass, 2004.

Cooper, J. "Educational MUVES: Virtual Learning Communities." *Interface: The Journal of Education, Community, and Values,* December 2003, http://bcis.pacificu.edu/journal/2003/09/cooper/cooper.php. Retrieved May 15, 2005.

Cunliffe, R. "Pilot Study into the Use and Usefulness of Instant Messaging Within an Educational Context." Paper presented at Statistics Education and the Communication of Statistics, Sydney, Australia, 2005.

Dede, C., and Ketelhut, D. "Designing for Motivation and Usability in a Museum-Based Multi-User Virtual Environment." 2003, http://muve.gse.harvard.edu/muvees2003/documents/DedeKetelMUVEaera03final.pdf. Retrieved June 3, 2005.

DeSanctis, G., and Gallupe, R. B. "A Foundation for the Study of Group Decisions Support Systems." *Management Science,* May 1987, *33*(5), 589–610.

Elton, L., & Johnston, B. "Assessment in Universities: A Critical Review Assessment Research." York, U.K.: LTSN Generic Centre, 2002.

Fahlman, S. "Smiley Lore:-)." http://www-2.cs.cmu.edu/~sef/sefSmiley.htm. Retrieved June 13, 2005.

Graham, C., Cagiltay, K., Lim, B., Craner, J., and Duffy, T. "Seven Principles of Effective Teaching: A Practical Lens for Evaluating Online Courses." *Technology Source,* March/April 2001, reprinted at http://sln.suny.edu/sln/public/original.nsf/0/b495223246cabd6b85256a090058ab98?OpenDocument. Retrieved June 20, 2005.

Haefner, J. "Opinion: The Importance of Being Synchronous." *Academic Writing,* April l9, 2000, http://wac.colostate.edu/aw/teaching/haefner2000.htm. Retrieved May 1, 2005.

Harvard Graduate School of Education (GSE). "Multi-User Virtual Environment Experiential Simulator." Harvard Graduate School of Education (GSE), July 27, 2003, http://muve.gse.harvard.edu/muvees2003. Retrieved June 30, 2005.

Hofmann, J. *The Synchronous Trainer's Survival Guide: Facilitating Successful Live and Online Courses, Meetings, and Events.* San Francisco: Pfeiffer, 2003.

Hofmann, J. *Live and Online: Tips, Techniques, and Ready-to-Use Activities for the Virtual Classroom.* San Francisco: Pfeiffer, 2004a.

Hofmann, J. "Teaching Online Is Like Teaching After Lunch." *T+D Magazine,* January 2004b, *58*(1), 19–21.

Hourcade, J., and Bauwens, J. "Cooperative Teaching: The Renewal of Teachers." *Clearing House,* May/June 2001, *74*(5), 242.

Juwah, C. "Using Peer Assessment to Develop Skills and Capabilities." *USLDA Journal,* Jan. 2003, *17*(1), http://www.usdla.org/html/journal/JAN03_Issue/article04.html. Retrieved June 1, 2005.

Kimura, B. "Welcome Address." TCC 2002 Online Conference, May 21, 2002, http://makahiki.kcc.hawaii.edu/tcc/tcon02/greetings/kimura.html. Retrieved May 1, 2005.

Knowles, M. "Fostering Competence in Self-Directed Learning." In R. M. Smith and Associates (eds.), *Learning to Learning Across the Lifespan.* San Francisco: Jossey-Bass, 1990.

Krohn, F. "A Generational Approach to Using Emoticons as Nonverbal Communication." *Journal of Technical Writing & Communication,* 2004, *34*(4).

Ludwig-Hardman, S., and Dunlap, J. "Learner Support Services for Online Students: Scaffolding for Success." *International Review of Research in Open and Distance Learning,* April 2003, http://www.irrodl.org/content/v4.1/dunlap.html. Retrieved June 1, 2005.

Marsick, V., and Watkins, K. "Informal and Incidental Learning." New Directions for Adult and Continuing Education, No. 89, 25. San Francisco: Jossey-Bass, 2001.

McGoff, C. J., and Ambrose, L. "Empirical Information from the Field: A Practitioner's View of Using GDSS in Business." Proceedings of the Twenty-Fourth Annual Hawaii International Conference on Systems Sciences, 1991.

McIsaac, M., Blocher, J., Mahes, V., and Vrasidas, C. "Student and Teacher Perceptions of Interaction in Online Computer-Mediated Communication." *Educational Media International,* June 1999, *36*(2), 121.

Mehrabian, A. "Methods & Designs: Some Referents and Measures of Nonverbal Behavior. *Behavioral Research Methods and Instrumentation,* 1969, *1,* 203–207.

Palloff, R., and Pratt, K. *Building Learning Communities in Cyberspace.* San Francisco: Jossey-Bass, 1999.

Palloff, R., and Pratt, K. *Collaborating Online: Learning Together in Community.* San Francisco: Jossey-Bass, 2005.

Partnership for 21st Century Skills. "Learning for the 21st Century: A Report and Mile Guide for 21st Century Skills." Washington, D.C.: Partnership for 21st Century Skills, 2003, http://www.21stcenturyskills.org/images/stories/otherdocs/P21_Report.pdf. Retrieved May 1, 2005.

Piaget, J. *The Mechanisms of Perception.* New York: Routledge Kegan Paul, 1969.

Pumphrey, J., and Slater, J. "An Assessment of Generic Skills Needs." London: Department for Education and Skills, 2002. http://www.des.gov.uk/skillsdialoguereports/docs/SD13_Generic.pdf. Retrieved May 10, 2005.

Reinig, B., Briggs, R., and Nunamaker, J. "Flaming in the Electronic Classroom." *Journal of Management Information Systems,* Winter 1997–1998, *14*(3), 45.

Repplier, A., "The Luxury of Conversation." *Compromises.* Reprint Services Corp, 1904. Selected quotations available at http://education.yahoo.com/reference/quotations/quote/56250.

Russell, T. "No Significant Difference Phenomenon Web Site." 2002, http://www.nosignificant difference.org. Retrieved June 25, 2005.

Schullo, S. "Synchronous Distance Education Support Systems, Why Does USF Need One?" The TLT Group, 2003, http://www.tltgroup.org/CommunityConnectedness/SynchTools.htm. Retrieved June 30, 2005.

Shiu, E., and Lenhart, A. "How Americans Use Instant Messaging." Washington, D.C.: Pew Internet & American Life Project, September 1, 2004.

Tait, A. "Reflections on Student Support in Open and Distance Learning." *International Review of Research in Open and Distance Learning,* April 2003, http://www.irrodl.org/content/v4.1/tait_editorial.html. Retrieved June 2, 2005.

"Time Spent During Synchronous Meetings?" *DEOS-L: The Distance Education Online Symposium, The Pennsylvania State University,* thread 89, June 2005, http://lists.psu.edu/cgi-bin/wa?A1=ind0506&L=deos-l. Retrieved June 29, 2005.

Twigg, C. "Innovations in Online Learning: Moving Beyond No Significant Difference." Troy: Center for Academic Transformation, 2001.

WGBH/Boston. "The Telephone: Program Transcript." *The American Experience,* 1997, http://www.pbs.org/wgbh/amex/telephone/filmmore/transcript/index.html. Retrieved June 15, 2005.

Wikipedia. "Emoticon." http://en.wikipedia.org/wiki/Emoticon. Retrieved June 15, 2005.

Yoong, P. "Assessing Competency in GSS Skills: A Pilot Study in the Certification of GSS Facilitators." Proceedings of the 1995 ACM SIGCPR Conference on Supporting Teams, Groups, and Learning, Nashville, 1995.

Index

84, 86, 87–89; virtual classroom and interactive Webcast preparation, 93. *See also* Learning activities; Virtual body language

Faculty. *See* Instructors

Fahlman, Scott, 78

Feedback: from instructors, 23–25; integrating into live sessions, 89–91; inviting pre- and post-event, 142; noting flickers on screen, 89; options for in recorded course postings, 47; polling and quizzing tools for, 45

File-sharing tools, 41–42

Finn, Barney, 36

Firewalls, 145

Flickers on screen, 89

Focusing synchronous events: managing side activities, 73–74; neutralizing distractions, 74–75; setting ground rules, 70–73, 89–90, 97; specifying and maintaining focus, 70, 71; technical means for, 72–73

Full duplex, 38

Further reading resources, 133–134

G

Gamson, Zelda, 15–16, 18, 21, 23, 26, 28, 30, 32

Gauging group *Gestalt* in synchronous interactions, 82–83

Godfrey, Neale, 85

Good practices. *See* Principles for undergraduate instruction

Grading, 20

Ground rules for synchronous events, 70–73, 89–90, 97

Group support systems (GSS), 63, 64

Guest experts: as facilitating role, 87–88; real-time online sessions with, 10, 103, 118–121

H

Haefner, Joel, 23–24, 31

Half duplex, 38

Hofmann, Jennifer, 76

Hosking, Michael, 24–25

Hosting live online sessions, 66–67

Hourcade, Jack, 84

I

Immediacy, 75–76

In-class online aids, 51, 53, 63–64

Informal learning opportunities, 19

Instant messaging (IM): defined, 34; as online learning venue, 51, 52, 54–55

Instruction: misconceptions about synchronous, 135–139; principles for good practice in, 15–16; scheduling synchronous, 140–142; served by synchronous interaction, 3; synchronous language, 17, 31–32. *See also* Principles for undergraduate instruction

Instructors: accessibility to learners, 16–18; assessing learners online, 11–13, 20; calling online sessions, 5; collaborating with partners in different time zones, 142; communicating expectations, 28–30; hosting synchronous sessions, 66–67; importance of, 65–66; making synchronous compact with learners, 5–7; modeling time on task, 26; peer cooperation for, 20; prompt feedback from, 23–25; recognizing learner's online cues, 82–83; respecting diverse talents and learning styles, 30–32, 74; as ringmaster, 69–75; sparking appreciation for subject, 7–8; synchronous certification for, 133; using breakout rooms, 46–47. *See also* Facilitating real-time learning

course maps, 44; polling and quizzing, 45; questions to ask before buying synchronous, 143–146; recording and playback of live audio and video, 47; simulated online environments, 48; slide showing, 43; text-based, 34; virtual whiteboards, 41–42; Web tours, 44
Troubleshooting technical crises, 94–98
Tutoring checklist for virtual sessions, 94
Twenty Questions activity, 117
Twigg, Carol, 39
Typing in real-time learning, 136

U

Upgrades for synchronous tools, 145

V

Venues. *See* Learning venues; Organizing synchronous venues
Versions of synchronous tools, 146
Video: conveying body language with, 83–84, 85; expectations for synchronous venues with, 137–138; factors effecting quality of live, 40; online tools, 39–40; questions to ask before buying tools for, 143–144; recording and playback of live sessions, 47
Virtual body language: benefits of nonverbal cues, 77–78; emoticons and abbreviations for, 78–80; exchanging nonverbal cues, 76–77; immediacy and, 75–76; judging learner's state of mind, 82–83; polling as proxy for body language, 80–82; video for, 83–84, 85
Virtual classroom: as online learning venue, 51, 53, 58–59; preparing for, 93–94
Virtual environments. *See* Learning venues; Synchronous interactions
Virtual office/meeting room, 51, 52, 57–58
Virtual reference desk: as activity, 128; as online learning venue, 51, 52, 56–57
Voice activation for video participation, 40
Voice over Internet Protocol (VoIP), 37
VOW (voice of the Web) role, 87

W

Web: factors effecting quality of video over, 40; sites on synchronous learning, 133–134; Web tour tools, 44
Webcasting: as interactive learning venue, 51, 53, 59–61; preparing for interactive, 93–94; streaming broadcasts, 37–38, 61–63
Whiteboards: about, 41–42; questions before buying, 144

Y

Yoong, Pak, 65